GRUMPY OLD WOMEN

GRUMPY OLD WOMEN
JUDITH HOLDER

Dedicated to women of a certain age everywhere, who are so often misunderstood, and to my own two trainee Grumpy Old Women, Siena and Ellen Parker.

This book is published to accompany the television series entitled *Grumpy Old Women*, which was first broadcast in 2005. The series was produced by Liberty Bell Productions for BBC Television.
Executive producer: Stuart Prebble
Written and produced by Judith Holder

Published by BBC Books, BBC Worldwide Limited, Woodlands, 80 Wood Lane, London W12 0TT

ISBN 0 563 52253 4

Commissioning editor: Shirley Patton Project editor: Sarah Reece
Copy editor: Trish Burgess Designer: Linda Blakemore
Illustrator: Susan Hellard Production controller: Alix McCulloch

Set in Baskerville and Strayhorn
Printed and bound in Great Britain by CPI Bath

For more information about this and other BBC books, please visit our website on www.bbcshop.com or telephone 08700 777 001.

Contents

Foreword

WHEN I WAS ASKED to be part of the *Grumpy Old Women* TV series I wondered just how much grump I had in me, but once the camera started rolling I realized I couldn't stop – just about everything and anything niggles the hell out of me. But surely this wasn't meant to happen to us – we were the first generation to be liberated, indulge in a spot of free love, put flowers in our hair. And now look at us – mad as hell … but rather cute and irresistible with it.

The average grumpy day begins when I leave the house for work. I get to the end of my drive and I can't turn on to the road, because the geniuses who only live to blight my local traffic system have placed a bus stop directly opposite the existing stop, on the narrowest part of a busy-to-busting main road, on a curve, 400 metres from the worst traffic lights in North London. Not a good start.

Twenty minutes later I'm at last on my way to rehearsals in Waterloo. I will be in reverse for much of the journey as I'm faced down by one hideous, fuel-guzzling, air-polluting, four-wheel-drive people carrier after another. Needless to say, the roads are peppered with temporary lights, gaping holes, orange cones by the thousand and not a single working workman anywhere to be seen.

My next grumpy moment occurs in the lavatory, where I become engaged in hand-to-hand combat with an industrial-sized toilet-roll applicator the size of Pavarotti. There I am, bent over, my hand curved back on itself like a Balinese temple dancer, flailing away at a perforated piece of paper I can neither see nor reach.

During the day my grumpiness increases. I can take any amount of Anglo Saxon expletives, but what I can't tolerate is someone telling me that I'll be 'sat' over there, as if I were a plant pot, or pronouncing the letter 'h' as 'haitch'. Aaargh! Or waiters waving 14-inch pepper pots in front of my nose – as if I want 14 inches of anything. Or baseball caps worn back to front by the large and the aged – they're not dumb enough worn forwards? Which only leaves television and this foreword isn't long enough to house my despair.

There is a bright spot on my frowning horizon: the truly marvellous, the truly cathartic, TV series *Grumpy Old Women*, which is made for women like you and me – a little bit older, and maybe a little bit fatter, but inside still the eighteen-year-old we were when we forced ourselves into a pair of hot pants. So here's to *Grumpy Old Women* – God bless her and all who sail in her …

Yours, incredibly grumpily,
Maureen Lipman

Introduction

GRUMPY OLD WOMEN are a little bit older than they were, they're a little bit fed up – quite a lot fed up, actually – and this book is dedicated to this hitherto silent majority of women of a certain age who find the whole business of being a grown-up infinitely harder than they had imagined. Age itself is irrelevant. They may look a teeny bit middle-aged on the outside, but on the inside they are the young, fragile and entirely irresistible women they were in their 20s. They may not wear thongs or sex-kitten bikinis any more, but it doesn't mean that deep down they aren't every bit as gorgeous and irresistible as they were all those years ago. This book is for those wonderful women – they might be 30, or 40 or 50 or much older – who share a special serenity and wisdom that means that they are nearly always right. They nearly always know best … and I am proud to be their self-appointed form captain.

This book is also for the people who are lucky enough to live with women like us. It can be their guide map to understanding the true depths and beauty of our (sometimes not apparent to the naked eye) charm, intuition, affection and sheer bloody wonderfulness.

So how does it feel to be a Grumpy Old Woman? Well, for a start, it seems like only yesterday that you were raving it up to 10cc and the Bay City Rollers, only five minutes since you were scrutinising the problem page in *Jackie* magazine to try to glean more information about the docking procedure of sexual intercourse, and no time at all since you were doing your hair in flick-backs like Charlie's Angels. But then look what happened – you got older and a little bit fatter, and suddenly you got grumpy. Boy, you got grumpy. And now just about everything gets you in a bad mood. Some days you are so mad that you walk past a pigeon and feel like giving it a good boot up the backside for no reason at all; if you see someone up a ladder, the idea of kicking it away from under them appeals for no reason other than that it would make you feel momentarily better; and if you were on *Who Wants to Be a Millionaire*, you'd agree in rehearsal to wave when they introduced you, but then sit on your hands when it came to doing it for real. Just out of spite.

You thought that you were supposed to mellow as you got older, to become mature, serene and all-knowing, but the truth is that these days you are boiling mad, and if you could *find* the rolling pin, you'd brandish it in traffic, and clip people round the ear with it when they annoyed you. Which is all the time. Everyone. And everything. It's just as well they don't sell guns at Argos.

Just in case you're not sure whether you, or the woman you are buying this book for, is a Grumpy Old Woman – here are some of the things to look out for:

SIGNS OF BEING A GRUMPY OLD WOMAN

- Your bra size is practically a telephone number, and you now shop in the underwear department from hell.
- If you sat on a beanbag, you might need to call the emergency services to get you out.
- You say to people, 'That shows my age,' and they no longer contradict you.
- You are the litter police.
- Shop assistants cower in fear as you storm up to their counter to return shoddy goods.

- Market researchers in the street with stupid clipboards ignore you – you've been ignoring *them* for years, anyway.
- Little bits of your face start to sag and give you that really grumpy look often seen on the sort of women who push their way in at jumble sales and get all the bargains.
- You have to put your reading glasses on the end of your nose, and glare over them like the headmistress in *Please Sir*.
- You remember *Please Sir*.
- You are plucking your facial hair on an hourly basis. It's all right for men – they're *meant* to have a moustache.
- You complain a lot.
- You like a nice fountain pen.
- You become a morning person.
- You start to enjoy pottering.
- You develop the Edward Heath double chin.
- You start collecting used margarine tubs and used plastic bags.
- Young men are afraid to be left alone with you lest you pounce.
- You like a slip-on shoe – saves all that bending.
- You find Terry Wogan less annoying.
- You order your first pleated skirt from a catalogue.
- You are secretly rather pleased that your daughter has an orthodontic brace that looks like part of the waste disposal unit because – let's be honest – it makes you look a bit better.
- If you wore a thong, you might look like a Sumo wrestler.
- You buy attention-seeking bags and shoes on the basis that they do them in your size, and send out what you believe are fun and funky image messages.
- Easy-care fabrics start to appeal.
- Your pubes start to go a bit straggly, a bit grey, a bit sparse.

- In the (very) unlikely event that you went pony trekking, everyone else would be given normal ponies and then they'd bring out a carthorse big enough to tow a juggernaut for you. That's code for 'you now have a fat arse'.

THINGS THAT BUG GRUMPY OLD WOMEN

These things are just the tip of the iceberg you understand – a full list obviously wouldn't fit into a book, dur …

- Grumpy Old Men. Women have every reason to be grumpy. Men do not. Deciding whether to comb over, whether to tuck the shirt under or over the beer belly, or experiencing some frustration with superglue is about as bad as it gets for men. (Mind you, superglue *is* annoying.)
- People who say 'bear with me two seconds' when you know they are going to be 15 minutes.
- Stupid Americanisms that have polluted our language, such as people asking the waiter if they can 'get' the soup to start … What do they mean? They want to go into the kitchen and get it themselves?
- Things that claim to be 'home-made' or 'farm fresh' when you know they are the entire opposite, as in they have come from the freezer in the cash and carry.
- Stupid words at the end of a name that are supposed to convince us that something is hugely better than it was. Our Jobcentre has just been renamed Jobcentreplus – the only difference being that there are now laminated floors, a lot of yellow and green paint, and fewer staff to help you.
- Coffee-vending machines that have run out of cups but still take your money while pouring all your coffee down the plughole.

- Needless and pointless signs that are supposed to be helpful, such as 'Warning – deep water' situated right next to the sea, or 'Beware – tripping hazard' on a perfectly visible step, or 'May contain nuts' on a whole nut bar of chocolate, but which are really only there to protect someone from litigation.
- Sellotape. Especially the behaviour of Sellotape during the Christmas period.
- Child-proof aspirin bottle tops that you need a child to help you to open.
- Stupid pyramids of apples that people put on counters at pretentious beauty parlours – not because they think you might like an apple, but just because they think it looks chic and expensive. I always help myself to the bottom one …
- Pointless stickers on the backs of cars. I saw one today that said 'Twins on Board'. Good job you told me, otherwise I'd have slammed into the back of you.
- Jane Asher and her stupid marvellous cakes.

If you're still not sure whether you, or the woman you are buying this book for, embody the requisite degree of grumpiness, listen out for some of the following.

GRUMPY OLD WOMEN TEND TO SAY …

- Is it me or is it hot in here?
- I shan't be coming here again.
- I can remember those flared trousers first time around.
- *How* much?
- What a rip off.
- It's a disgrace.
- What's for lunch?

- I want to talk to the manager.
- You're too young to be the manager.
- Bonking (when describing others – obviously).
- I'm 'popping' out. (Only middle-aged people 'pop'. It's very Valerie Singleton).
- I could murder a nice cup of tea.
- Let's have a sit down.
- Cheerio.
- Cheers.
- Struth.
- Hasn't it been cool for the time of year?
- The hit parade.
- Spending a penny.
- Naughty but nice.
- We can't go on meeting like this.
- Whoops.
- Right you are.

GRUMPY OLD WOMEN SPEND LITTLE TIME …

- Sicking up in the street.
- Asking the doctor for the morning-after pill – but it might be a laugh to show up at the surgery one busy morning and ask.
- Three-in-a-bed sessions.
- Snogging in public.
- Lighting farts (in public).
- Putting bollards on the tops of statues – although, interestingly, Grumpy Old Women would be the last people the police would suspect – neat.
- Wearing T-shirts that say 'Fancy a shag' or 'All I want is a blow job'.

But perhaps we shouldn't be putting such wicked thoughts into respectable middle-aged women's heads.

CHAPTER ONE

From hot pants to hot flushes

YOU STILL FEEL YOUNG. You still feel like you did when you were about 18. OK, so you know a lot more than you did: you know that the chocolate-vending machines in Tube stations never work; you know that two days after chucking something out, you find a use for it and wish you'd kept it. Those sorts of pearls of wisdom are among the benefits of age. However, trying to crack the business of being a grown-up is infinitely trickier.

Sometimes, even at my age, I still feel like I'm preparing for life proper to begin, still trying to get things balanced and orderly so that I can begin living Life with a capital L – being a domestic goddess and a successful woman about town rolled into one. Probably with a house by the sea and matching bed linen, where the sun shines every day. But then John Lennon got it right when he said, 'Life is what happens when you're planning other things'. Real life is about putting the washing away, managing the nine-to-five routine, and waking up in the middle of the night wondering whether you left the oven on.

I still feel like I did when my life was just beginning, like I did when I started at university, like I did when I was driving my first car, but I look in the mirror and see someone who is very evidently grown up and way past that time. Grown right up and over the other side of the hill. I can't believe I'm now the age my parents were at their silver wedding anniversary, when I thought they looked about 95. That night I saw them kiss – the only time I saw them kiss – and thought to myself it was disgustingly inappropriate at *their age*. Now, two minutes later, here I am the same age myself.

So let's start with some of the physical attributes that go with the territory. Some of the things that we see in the mirror or in the holiday photos that cheese us off and get us very grumpy indeed.

MIDDLE-AGE SPREAD

My entire body is turning into my mother's, or Judy Finnegan's. I now look so old that if I was stupid enough to go into a nightclub, people would assume I was an undercover police-woman. WPC Menopausal. If I got on to the dance floor and strutted my stuff, people would run for cover, averting their eyes in horror, like in an Alfred Hitchcock film. Just like my mother, every bit of my body is either sagging, or bulging, or both. I'm sprouting some of those bobbly warty things on my nose and chin that look just like the ones they sell in fancy-dress shops for Halloween parties. Is there any bit of my body that doesn't need a spot of structural repair? Even my feet are getting all idiosyncratic: my toes are growing in odd directions, my toenails are so hard and horny that I've had to buy a pair of those nail scissors that could cut whole chickens in half, and open-toed sandals are a no-go area. Perhaps that's why God invented pop socks – perfect camouflage as well as natural contraceptives (being guaranteed passion-killers).

And my boobs … Oh – my – God! It's like someone is inflating them with the thing we take camping to blow up the sleeping-bags. Slowly but surely they expand every month.

The only bras that fit now have pulleys, ropes and hooks, and are built by civil engineers. Bras for Grumpy Old Women today, suspension for the Forth Bridge tomorrow. My bras now look like the kind of thing Hattie Jacques would have hung up in *Carry on Camping* … If I did try to burn my bra these days, I might have to call the fire brigade.

And then there's knickers – sorry, I mean pants. High leg, low leg, pull in, pull out … what's a middle-aged girl to do for the best? Corrective underwear is what, as long as you are not going on a hot date. Some chance! And thongs, whose idea were they? Not a middle-aged woman's, that's for sure. Middle-aged women and thongs – not a good look. Think Sumo wrestler … So don't say you weren't warned. Although I see they've now brought out the 'control thong', with an industrial-strength elasticated panel down the front, which pulls you in so dramatically that it makes you walk at a 45-degree angle and pushes the rest of you out at the back, giving you a neat rear-view shelf for keeping things on – which is handy.

I tried thongs for a bit, and I thought they were marvellous because you've got no line, no visible panty line, which is kind of cheesy. And so I went into thongs in a big way. And I can't wear them now because I wore them so much I gave myself galloping anal itch.

Dillie Keane

No, I don't think I would've worn thongs even when I was young and trying very hard. No, that's ridiculous. You might just as well go without knickers at all.

Annette Crosbie

So popular are thongs (for reasons that totally escape me) that scientists are apparently working on the maternity thong. Just pause and think of that for a moment – picture the ads on billboards – I suspect they'll cause accidents, or cardiac arrests.

All those lovely sex-kitten cute underwear shops with teeny-weeny bras and fancy strappy knickers and sexy-bitch ranges are no longer for me. I imagine if I went into one of those shops they'd say they didn't have anything in my size without even looking. Just as well I'm not thinking of having an affair, isn't it? It would have to be seriously dark. Not that I'd ever really have the nerve. I could never pluck up the courage to buy the condoms. Even though they are tantalisingly near the till at Asda. It would be just my luck for Brown Owl to take over on the checkout as I sneaked them under the cauli.

Everything's going to pot – even my knees are going all saggy and droopy, and never mind cellulite on the backs of my thighs – I now have it on the front too.

Facial hair is a real and constant battle. Some of us could give a Philoshave a run for its money.

The worst thing is a sudden shaft of sunlight and a mirror. And you think, 'My God, I've been walking around like the Forest of Dean'. If I were to lose my tweezers, I would die.

Nina Myskow

They're sort of individual. And a bit like 'Look at me, I'll just be growing here, on my own, and in a pubic style as well.'

Arabella Weir

Plucking and tweezing is simply not enough – it's the sheer volume of pubic styles, and they're not wispy ones, but great blooming dark things that look like fuse wire – so you have several choices: you can go to the beautician's every week for the foreseeable future and have some hideous course of electrolysis or laser treatment that will clog up your diary and set you back hundreds of pounds, or you can buy one of the home waxing kits they sell at Boots. I followed the instructions to a T, but even I could see that if I got this wrong I could be walking round with first-degree burns on my top lip during the annual sales conference. I put it in the microwave as instructed, walked oh-so-carefully upstairs to the bedroom mirror with it, and gently pasted it on my upper lip and chin with a stick that looked like the ones supplied with ice-cream tubs at the pictures. Trouble is, I couldn't get the stuff off, and then it all hardened, which it's not supposed to, and it took me a good hour of excruciating pain to pick it all off bit by bit with a pair of tweezers. There was no big satisfying rip like it promises on the packet. I think I managed to nuke about three hairs after hours of agony, and ended up with a bright-red top lip that looked like I'd drunk too much Ribena. Great.

WEIGHTY MATTERS

Middle age, of course, also affects your middle. The old midriff bulge makes an appearance, and you get a nasty paunch. If you're wearing something floaty people glance down at it and wonder – just for a second – whether it might be that you're pregnant – but then realize the statistical improbability and assume (more accurately) you just like your food too much. You wear a pair of shorts and now they ride up your crotch and your legs rub together. I suppose you should have known better than to wear shorts at all. Your upper arms go all Mrs Mills and flop about when you wave someone goodbye or shake out the duvet. So unless you can set aside an hour's weightlifting every day, sleeveless T-shirts are out.

And all this structural repair that your body needs *takes* so long. Even brushing your teeth is high maintenance. You can't just brush your teeth and get on with your day; you have to get out all the surgical implements the hygienist flogged you – flosses, tapes, little brushes for between your crowns, buffers and pokers to get your gums in shape and to maintain all your root canal work. By the time you've tweezed out your beard and done all the dental work, you can count on at least an hour before you even get downstairs in the morning. Then there's your corns to scrape, your yoga to do and your eyebrows to pluck. You're left with only about half an hour a day to *achieve* anything. You remember – stones ago – when a visible panty line was as depressing as things got? What you would give for that to be your major problem now?

None of this was going to happen to you. But then it does, not because of anything you consciously do or don't do. It just happens. And with luck you are married to a Grumpy Old Man with man-breasts and sticky-out hairs on his shoulders and it doesn't seem so damned important.

It's not as if you can just knuckle down to a big box of Quality Street and turn into Peggy Mount, as your mother did, with no one batting an eyelid. These days you have to try to retain your figure by spending hours in the gym, then spend hours at the hairdresser's trying to re-create your natural (or I should say original) hair colour (assuming you can still remember it). People say, 'You look well', which is code for 'You look a bit fat', and you buy those big necklaces to cunningly divert people's attention from your larger boobs and chin. When you have your photo taken you have to suck your tummy in. And when they come back you think you forgot to.

Wrinkles you were expecting, but your face starts to go all saggy round the jowls, you get battle-scar pot marks and splodges on your skin and that grumpy look begins to take hold. On a bad day you stare at yourself in the mirror and think that people might say you have the face you deserve, which is undoubtedly not a very pretty one. You could spend your entire salary on skin care.

Thank God for beauty products because at least they give you hope. Even if they do nothing for you, you can sort of slam the box to your forehead and think it's helping. And it has to be expensive stuff because if it's cheap stuff, it won't work. I'm not interested in cheap stuff. I don't care if it's all packaging, that's fine by me. Just as long as it sells me a dream.

Nina Myskow

Time was when a tub of Nivea was as complicated as it got. Now you have to buy cleansers, toners, night cream, day cream, stabilisers and all manner of quasi-scientific products that sound as though they could double as biological weapons. You are now so cynical about all these skincare products that cost about £100 a pop that you wonder whether a dollop of

Flora on both cheeks might be just as effective. You don't know what to do for the best. If only Valerie Singleton were still on *Blue Peter* she'd have known what to do: probably would have had a cunning plan with some sticky-backed plastic.

I don't actually inhabit my body any more. At some point somebody came along, body snatched, gave me this. It's the kind of body I used to look at on beaches and think, 'Goodness me, how does that happen? How could you let yourself go like that?' That's how it happens – it just happens.

Kathryn Flett

You consider drastic measures to hold back the tide of physical decay. You buy one of those abdominal exercisers that sit on the bedroom floor and trip people up and snag their ankles, and eventually work their way into the corner and then into the spare room, before finally being advertised in the local paper and then taken down to the car boot sale.

You could go in for some botox, or try never to smile or laugh again (might be surprisingly achievable, in fact) to ensure no more wrinkles appear, or spend your entire savings on having it all snipped and sucked away. I blame *Heat* magazine.

Even your hair – in fact, especially your hair – goes all horrid and frizzy and grey and washed out. Whatever products you buy, and there are plenty to choose from, you get the fly-away Camilla Parker Bowles bouffant hair from hell – not a good look. The only way to look remotely presentable is to have it 'done' like your mother did – to go to the hairdresser twice a week and have it pulled and clamped and straightened into behaving. But we don't have time for this, so we do it ourselves and manage to blow dry one side just fine, but the other does its own thing and frizzes up, so that we look like we've plugged ourselves into the mains.

The grey hair advances at such a pace that you have to give up going to the salon – to use that marvellously middle-aged word – and dye your own roots at home. Trouble is, Grumpy Old Women are not known for their patience and attention to detail. They don't have time to read instructions on anything. You get the packet home and it has to be on your hair within 30 seconds, the keys still swinging in the front door. Reading the instructions is far too much fuss and bother, and would involve getting your specs on, so, like everything else, you do it at 100 miles an hour and don't notice that the instructions say you have to wear protective gloves, or that it has to cook in the microwave for 15 seconds first (depending on the wattage of your microwave, not that you've ever got time to look into that sort of malarky … Don't be silly – too busy).

It's the same story when you decorate. You have to be getting paint on the walls within three minutes of walking through the door with the can of paint. No time to prepare surfaces or read instructions; barely even time to cover up the beds or carpets. Everything has to be now, immediate, because Grumpy Old Women are the most impatient people on earth. They are running out of time fast, and boy, do they know it. Naturally, it means that you end up with bright-red hair the colour of a postbox, or you get a stipple effect on the radiators instead of gloss white, or you microwave the supper and it explodes, splattering the kitchen with chicken tikka that takes industrial cleaning to get rid of. See how much time you save?

And now that you are a bit older, a bit more middle-aged, what on earth are you supposed to wear? Everything in the shops – skinny little vests, hipster pants, sleeveless tops – is aimed at young people, and obviously isn't available in your size. Of course, there's a good reason for this: you'd look bloody stupid in it.

Now that I'm old [shopping for clothes has] become entirely frustrating because there is nothing for me to wear in the shops. Nothing. I mean, I'm not going to wear hipster pants, am I? If I wear hipster pants and I sit down, I'll shoot out the back of them. It's not on.

Germaine Greer

I find myself buying something simply because it's comfortable. And I think, 'That'll be practical', so I'll go home with a skirt of unspeakable ugliness, and I'll think, 'Oh that'll be quite nice. I could just dress it up with one of my cardigans.' But three weeks later you think, 'Why did I buy this?'

Dillie Keane

Or you can go for the trying-too-hard look of black leather trousers, or a clingy, low-necked top revealing leathery cleavage and too much bosom, but you end up looking like Bet Lynch. Avoid leopardskin or safari fabrics of any kind as they spell 'desperate'. Just a little tip I picked up. You'll thank me.

You could pick up and browse through one of the many catalogues that come through your door from companies who have spotted that you are now middle-aged. Pages and pages of pleated skirts and cardigans, and acres of beige. Beige beige beige. As well as some nice china collectibles and stretch chintz sofa covers. You might huff and puff about them at first, but one day you will find something you fancy, something useful, such as a Venetian blind cleaner, and bingo, you're hooked. Anything that you can send off for without having to park the car and deal with shop assistants is a big plus, and with clothes you don't have to suffer the back view of yourself in the changing room mirror – oh, joy of joys. The trouble is that when the clothes arrive they never fit, and they never look like they're made of easy-care acrylic in the photos. You are then forever on the phone to returns and refunds, carefully packing them up, then queuing at the post office to return them all, and making sure they are credited to your Visa account when the statement comes through a month later. After all that, parking and going into the changing room begins to feel relatively convenient by comparison.

Shoes also become a nightmare, because suddenly you can't do high heels, what with the corns, the bad back, the bunions and the sheer exhaustion of it all. And then, when you do go for it, and you leave the Eccos at home and put some swanky heels on, you look like a drag queen, wobbling about because you're not used to them.

Unfortunately, exercise now has to form part of your daily routine. You start joining the early-morning swimming brigade to keep in some sort of acceptable shape, and also to feel less stiff and help the old aches and pains. But one day you can't make the early morning, and get there in the evening – just in time for the over-50s session. You'd like a swim, but wonder whether anyone will notice you are way under 50. You give it a go anyway, and approach the woman behind the counter – the one you dislike. One of the ones you dislike. Never got her mind on the job, that girl. People drown right under her nose and she's still thinking about what to wear on Saturday night. Cow. I bet when the going gets tough and the loos need hosing down, she's not the one chasing the turd round with the hosepipe. The sort of girl who is never there when you need her would be my reading of the situation. Not an attractive quality in a lifeguard.

So she's on the till. 'Swim please,' I say. No trouble so far. She hasn't actually looked up, so it doesn't count. 'Have you got any towels left?' I ask, making her look at me, and hoping that she is suddenly going to say, 'Now there's no way you're over 50.' She looks. She makes no comment. Not even, 'You do know it's the over-50s session, don't you ?' Do you know what she said ? Do you *know* what she said? 'I have got some towels but they're not very big – will you be able to manage?' I've decided to watch her very carefully from now on and plan to get her involved next time I swim past an unpleasant plaster that needs fishing out.

Once in the pool with the over-50s, of course, your mood lifts. My fellow swimmers gaze admiringly at me as I walk to the poolside with a positively youthful spring in my step. Once in the water, the flirting is tangible – men loitering in the shallow end waiting for me to push off for my next Olympic-style length. Well, length anyway. The only problem is that they are all over 60, but at least their varicose veins are hidden under the water.

The women are a different story … With their rubber flip-flops and drawstring wash-bags containing little plastic boxes of Pears soap, they were giving me the sort of look that seems to ask, 'How does she look so good at 50? OK, so her body has gone to pot, and she looks a bit rough around the eyes, but I wonder where she buys her skin-care from. What kind of HRT is she taking? We haven't seen her at line-dancing yet, and let's hope she doesn't start coming.'

If only the men were still up to it. Might be worth trying to wear a few of them out.

Sometimes all this effort spent on trying to hold back the tide of decay seems like a total waste of time. It's not even that anyone else cares two hoots what I look like now. No one even seems to notice how much older and fatter I've become, as I am now entirely invisible. Even those ghastly market researchers with clipboards in the shopping centre have started to ignore me. I only noticed it the other day. For years I have been avoiding *them* – pushing past their sad little ambush, mouthing, 'Too busy, sorry.' But when I think about it my invisibility has happened gradually. First they started to make less of a bee-line for me, looked less devastated if they didn't nail me. Now they don't even bother to stop me at all. I actually went right up to one the other day and, to give her a shock, asked her if she knew the way to the local Ann Summers shop. Of course, she just *told* me. Cow.

Now you are so invisible that when you ask someone, 'How do I look?' they gaze at you pityingly and say, 'fine', while thinking, 'like it matters?' To anyone at all. Even my Grumpy Old Man finds me invisible. I suppose he might notice if I had a hand grenade stuck on my forehead, but probably only if it went off.

Of course sometimes being invisible is a godsend.

There are tremendous upsides to being invisible. You can observe, you can watch. Life is more interesting. When you're self-involved and you see yourself centre stage all the time, you're in agonies of self-consciousness, you're really concerned: How do I look? How do I sound? It's wonderful not to care about that any more.

Germaine Greer

You can nip out to the chippy in your old anorak and some slippers and no one will bat an eyelid. Except when you do, it's sod's law you will bump into someone you want to impress – your boss, or your boss's boss – and now the anorak and the slippers feel like a terrible idea. So you cross the road and stare into the dry cleaner's window, pretending you've found something fascinating, and they come right up to you and gush, 'We thought it was you!'

It's not just the way you look that's a problem: your joints start to stiffen up, and you need a bit of momentum to get yourself out of chairs; you pick things up off the floor with more huffing and puffing, and those funny picky-uppy things that litter collectors use to pick up rubbish start to seem like a good idea; or you just leave stuff on the floor because you can't be bothered to pick it up. You have to sit down to put your socks on – none of this balancing on one leg nonsense any more. You can forget pole-dancing.

You have to buy some reading specs, which are a total nuisance. You fiddle around in your handbag for them, have to balance them on the end of your nose because they make you feel sick otherwise, but you can't see a thing without them. You can't even read the numbers on your mobile without fannying around with your specs. Of course, it would be easy if you bought a chain to put them round your neck, but come on – you have some pride. Who wants to look like Larry Grayson?

ALL CHANGE

As if all this wasn't enough to get you down, the menopause or 'the change' starts to rear its ugly, unfashionable head. Your period's late, which of course you don't notice for ages since the PMT now seems to run back to back from one end of the month to the other with only the briefest period of sanity in the middle. You take yourself off to the doctor and he says, 'How old are you now?' as if it's not in the notes in front of him. 'Forty-five' you say. 'When did your mother start the change?' Oh – my – God. We're not talking outrageously late pregnancy at all; rather, we are talking the start of the change. As a result, you leave with some HRT, not a pregnancy testing kit.

Suddenly periods seem so desirable, so happening, so cool. Makes you feel like spring-loading some tampons in your handbag to impress people, make them think you are still in the land of the living, still fertile. You had started to daydream about leaving a pregnancy testing kit casually in the bathroom cabinet, which would give Teenage Daughter a shock and wipe the smile off her face. You call Grumpy and sob down the phone to him about wanting to have babies again. He misunderstands and comes home with enough condoms to last (you) till the end of the year. Not the best idea in the circumstances, but hey, he could have gone mad and bought a whole ten-pack.

I suppose all the signs were there: the mood swings are getting a touch violent – one minute you are hurling plates at other members of the family (some with food still on) and the next you see some soppy article in *Woman's Weekly* about a child dying of liver cancer and you are a hopeless soggy mess on the sofa in need of group hugs and all sorts of embarrassing nonsense. Now it's sounding like we're difficult to live with or something. It has to be said that some women do go a bit bonkers as they hit middle age: they start to hang out at Cliff Richard concerts, or get front-row seats to see David Essex at the panto, then queue up at the stage door to get his autograph. I rest my case.

And the odd hot flush starts to happen – you get all hot and bothered over nothing at all.

I do get hot. Sometimes I think, 'Oh, I can smell the menopause on me.'
You know, it's kind of BO and Prozac and furniture polish.

Jenny Eclair

But undoubtedly the worst thing about turning into the middle-aged woman from hell is that you are turning into you know who – the one person you dread turning into …
your mother.

SIGNS OF BECOMING YOUR MOTHER

- You get out of a chair like she does.
- You enjoy a nice sit down like she does.
- You find yourself asking your daughter where her friends live, not out of any real interest, but in order to establish how middle class they are.

- You wipe cutlery in restaurants before using it.
- You are fussy about the state of the tea towels in the kitchen.
- You pick out a top with a nice collar.
- You complain that new curtains don't have enough lining.
- You fuss about how you are going to get somewhere, and start to fret about where the nearest loo is.
- You buy some lavender soap.
- Someone buys you scented drawer liners, and instead of throwing them away in a fit of temper, you try them out and like them.
- You let food get mouldy in the fridge and say that sticking to sell-by dates is a waste of money.
- You get lazy with the housework and try a spot of dusting using the hairdryer. Result!

The list of similarities between you and your mother grows longer and longer. Like her, you can't sleep. You need five trips to the loo in the middle of the night. You can't drink tea or coffee too late because it keeps you awake. Then the bed has to be just right – not too low, not too high. You're fussy about the pillow size, and the way the duvet sits. You don't like draughts, or too much noise, or too much light. You can't sleep in. Even on New Year's Day, when everyone else is still asleep at 11 a.m., you've been awake since seven and have emptied the dishwasher and cleaned the kitchen by the time they all stagger down, fresh-faced and rested. Bastards.

You fiddle on with domestic chores and worry about getting behind with the ironing, just like she did. You like to be 'in front' which effectively (no, ultimately) means that on your deathbed there won't be any potatoes to peel or any outstanding ironing.

You start to forget. You forget people's names, sometimes

your own children's names. You know you know someone who is waving at you, but you have no idea who they are.

Just sometimes you bump into people and you think, 'You're my best friend, aren't you? I recognise you. Ooh, you're looking a bit old. What's your name?'

Jenny Eclair

You can't remember people's names. I'm saying, 'Oh, do you remember that actor? You know, the one who was in that film,' and then you can't remember the film's name, and, 'You know, he was married to … ' and you can't remember who he was married to. 'You know, the one who had the dreadful childhood and she was on that show,' and you can't remember the TV show she was on.

Nina Myskow

You walk into the pantry and forget what you went in there to get; you go upstairs and purposely open a cupboard but can't remember why.

The memory's going, so I go up and down the stairs a lot. I go upstairs, I remember something downstairs; I go down again, I forget what I'm doing. I go into the the garden, I forget what I'm there for. Then I have to stand in the same place and think, 'Why am I here?'

Michele Hanson

You have to write everything down on sad little lists as soon as a thought strikes you. You write shopping lists on the back of cereal packets and then forget to take them with you when you do go shopping. You keep forgetting your PIN number, so you work out some cunning code and put it in the back of your diary, then stand at the cash point, forget how the code works and the machine eats your card. Not that you have reached your mother's stage yet – she is so forgetful now that if she were at school, she would be in Special Needs.

To make it worse, in fact, your mother seems to be having so much more fun than you. What with her creative writing, watercolour classes and line dancing, she's on a packed schedule; then there's all the soaps to watch – and the omnibus on Sunday. If she does manage to help out, it has to be in the ad break. She's always on some off-peak holiday to Tenerife. Probably topless, wouldn't be surprised. I blame EasyJet. I thought she was supposed to be knitting squares for the Red Cross or running Meals on Wheels or something. These days she is very 'with it', as she puts it – never out of slacks. Even the children seem to think she is very *à la mode*. Where does that leave me?

It's all enough to make you feel like doing something really wicked and rebellious, to show the world you are not prepared to go quietly into old age – how about leaving your mother sitting near the checkouts at Asda and not going back to pick her up, or wearing one of those hideous slogan T-shirts that young people love and you disapprove of so much – 'Fancy a Shag?' Or you could whizz up and down the office corridor playing Special Olympics on your funny bad-back chair that you have to kneel on. That'd give everyone a shock – make them sit up and notice you.

I suppose there are some pros to getting older. You just don't give a monkey's what people think any more. In your teens and 20s, you used to talk about how embarrassing things were. Now it would take something monumental to embarrass you. You get changed on the beach into your cossie without even taking too much trouble about holding the towel. Of course, if it fell off and uncovered a considerable volume of white flabby flesh for all to see, it would be your children who would be embarrassed, not you. Joy.

CHAPTER TWO

Having it all

'HAVING IT ALL' was going to mean that we could have a career of our own as well as bring up the perfect family. I think I belong to one of the first generations that received this message. We didn't have to choose between a career and a family as our mothers did. We could and should do *both*. But 20 years on it now feels like we were sold down the river on the 'having it all' idea. The only 'all' we seem to have now is all the work.

Having it all was infinitely more complicated than it seemed because no one considered who was actually going to look after the children. Also no one factored in that most women are genetically programmed for motherhood, and once they feel they are not 'doing' motherhood as well as they want to, they feel deeply unhappy. More than that, more practical than that, having it all seems to mean that far from being effortlessly able to combine all the status and money of a career with bringing up emotionally rounded children (while still finding time for a weekly facial), we are trying to do everything single-handedly. Woman are multi-tasking in double figures, while men seem to be able to go to work and then come home again, end of story. Somehow we seem to have ended up with *double* the work.

None of this was supposed to happen to my generation …
we were going to be so much happier, so much more fulfilled
than our mothers could have dreamt of. We were the first
women to take the pill, be properly liberated, to have a career
and bring up the 2.4 children. We drove 2CVs, we went to
NCT classes, we decided to have it all. We staged sit-ins and
demos for all sorts of things – actually I can't really remember
what the demos were for now … We were going to change the
world. But it was always going to take more than a Kenwood
mixer and some Tupperware to change our lives significantly,
and now we are over 40 and a bit fatter, it feels like all that
struggle and liberation has been, well, forgotten.

We strove hard to get our careers in the first place. We had
to be as good as, if not better than, the next man. We got near
the top of the ladder, got used to earning our own money. It
made us feel good, gave us self-respect and self-esteem. But
then we got pregnant. Suddenly we realised that having babies

wasn't going be as simple as we thought. We kissed our babies' heads, we snuggled up, we fell in love with them. We spent eight months of our maternity leave bonding and feeling for the first time in our lives that what we were doing was really important ... then we had to go back to work. Get back to the careers that took us so long to get in the first place. Leave our precious darlings with baby-minders or nannies – nannies who weren't so keen to poach organic apples, or who didn't know exactly how our babies liked their duvet, or wouldn't sit with them while they nodded off. Nannies who just didn't do any of it as well or as lovingly as we did. And it was all so exhausting. Broken nights and then full-on, full-time working days. There are no easy answers. In Sweden they seem to have got it right: the State pays for mothers and fathers to take 18 months off to look after their kids. But then, who wants to live in Sweden?

There is huge pressure now on women to be economically active. Huge diminution of the importance of bringing up children. That's now regarded as a second-class occupation. That's been a very, very undesirable consequence of Women's Lib. It wasn't what we thought about when we thought of Women's Lib all those years ago.
                                                    Ann Widdecombe

Whether they work outside the home or not, all women of a certain age have mountains to get through. My life has become one long to-do list. Lists of all shapes and sizes tyrannise my life. It's not just that they are a way of keeping a record of what I have to do in any one day. They are an important measure of whether I am managing to achieve what I consider to be essential tasks. All day, every day, year in, year out, my to-do lists remind me that I have far too much to do and will never *ever* get it all done. I will never, ever get to the end of my lists.

I have become obsessive about them. I write one on a Monday morning that has enough tasks on it to keep an entire army busy for a month. I have silly systems, such as asterisking the ones I think are really, really important. Sometimes I asterisk a few that I know I can cross off very quickly to trick myself into thinking I've achieved a great deal by 9.10, when I have actually only managed to fill the dishwasher, iron a skirt and call the fishmonger. In the top right-hand corner of my work list is an extra list of domestic things that need doing during the working day too, such as:

> Change Teenage Daughter's doctor's appointment
> Ring orthodontist
> Take bra back to M&S
> Buy pipe cleaners for Youngest Daughter's DT session on Friday
> Order school swimming hat

However, I should say (because, apart from anything else, my boss will be reading this book) that I also have work things on my weekend and home lists. Because the thing about Grumpy Old Women is that they are shit-hot at organising, so things get done. Things get knocked into shape when women like us are on the case. Otherwise … well, the whole thing would fall into a complete shambles.

Women are expected to do everything, and a lot more than they used to. Because they're expected to go out to work, to do the shopping, to do the housekeeping, to do everything, to bring up the children. Everything.

Annette Crosbie

LIFE-SAVING LISTS

Inevitably, some things appear on my list on a Monday morning, and are carried forward from one day to another for weeks on end. It's usually something I don't want to do, and invariably something tricky. The one and only self-preservation tip I have learnt, having lived with lists for 40 years is that if you leave something on the list for long enough, it eventually self-destructs. Sooner or later the thing you thought was so important will either get so bad that someone else has to sort it out, or it simply doesn't bother you enough any more to do anything about it.

We all seem to be doing enough in any one day to have kept our parents busy for a month. And it's not just women who find themselves in this boat. When my husband had to go back to work just a couple of days after I'd given birth I felt lucky to be a woman. Lucky to be the person who has some sort of choice, albeit one with financial implications, about how much time I could spend with the kids when they were still in their total and utter gorgeous babyhood. The world still understands when a woman chooses to stay at home to look after the children; when a man does so the world still writes him off as a bit weird.

But it is undoubtedly true that my husband doesn't get so bogged down with as many to-do lists at home, which is not to say he doesn't do the chores I ask him to (well, eventually anyway). The fact is that it all matters much more to me, so I have the lists in my head, and my mind gets clogged up to bursting point with all the bits and bobs that need doing. All the stuff such as what we have in for packed lunches, what's in or not in the fridge, how much milk I ordered and whether the girls' trainers are clean enough to send them to school in.

But of course the crunch really comes when one of the

kids is running a temperature during the working day. Even though I am in an important meeting at work it's *my* mobile that the nanny has got keyed into her phone, not my husband's.

You can't have it all actually, not without a fungal infection appearing somewhere.

Jenny Eclair

It's absolutely amazing to me that women still believe that they can have it all. It's still a promise. It's an insane promise. I would've thought that it had been demonstrated amply over the last 30 years that you can't have it all.

India Knight

It's not just the *lists* that Grumpy Old Women, home-based or not, have to contend with day in, day out – it's the god-awful *muddle* at home that everyone else in the family ignores and that worsens on a daily basis. The piles of washing that I put neatly at the bottom of the stairs for people to take up with them and put away *never* go away; everyone wafts past as if the piles don't even register on their radar. You might get one lot put away, then someone messes up another room or leaves all the videos in a heap, or searches through a drawer and doesn't put it all back. The muddle – or trying to tame it – obviously features regularly on The List, often along the following lines.

> Sort airing cupboard
> Put things out for car boot sale
> Put ad in for bike, etc.
> Move dog food to garden shed

So, once again, women are undoubtedly their own worst enemies because all this stuff matters to us. If the beds aren't made when we leave home in the morning, or the Shreddies are still on the kitchen table when we get home at night it niggles and bothers and eats away at us all day. Consequently, there is about 2 per cent of our brain left to devote to other matters. Imagine what we would be like if we had all the time men have to do non-domestic things. We'd solve the Middle East crisis over a cup of coffee and run the Home Office while making tomorrow's packed lunches. Done. Sorted.

Women's magazines don't help – all those *Good Housekeeping* spreads on Delia Smith or Jane Asher that make you feel so inadequate, and so – well – in a muddle. *They* have beautifully organised houses that make yours look like the council tip. Then the Lakeland catalogue comes through the door, offering fabulous drawer dividers that keep your socks in cute individual housings. Here is your dream of coordinating scatter cushions and bedspreads, of opening the linen cupboard and finding Benetton-type arrangements of towels and sheets. You spend a weekend reorganising everyone's socks and sticking little labels in the airing cupboard, saying 'single towels', 'bath towels', 'flannels', 'guest towels' (ok, so you went a bit mad), and you gather everyone in the kitchen for a meeting and say you want to make a few changes around the house. They all concentrate in case you are about to tell them you are walking out, or you are reducing their pocket money, or only ever cooking organic fish pie from now on, no oven chips allowed. Then you say, 'It's about all the mess and clutter … there are going to be a few changes' and they promptly lose eye contact. Your partner shuffles about and so do the kids. They think it's another one of your mad schemes. You read out your list, going through it with a pointy thing and underlining requests, such as: 'Please, when you go to the bathroom and use a towel, can you put it back on the hook, rather than just leaving it on the floor and stepping over it?'

You have to restrain yourself from writing signs everywhere, such as: 'Please leave the bathroom how you found it', or 'Please turn off taps' lest you turn into a B&B landlady from hell.

The scary truth is that the only person who is bothered about the muddle, the only person who even has it on their radar is *you*. No one else even notices it. It clogs up your brain, and clutters up your waking thoughts, but in fact you are never, ever going to win the battle over the muddle. Get over it. With kids, an untidy partner and possibly a full-time job, you are never *ever* going to win. The muddle will always be there. Even if it is jammed into a cupboard out of sight, like all the holiday snaps you take and never get the chance to sort out or put in albums – except I think mothers cleverer than me put theirs in albums with cute (or not very cute, in fact) labels saying: 'When Jamie fell in the pool with all his clothes on', 'Sophie's 6th birthday, and we forgot the cake' – usually with a lot of exclamation marks at the end of them. Their albums are all lined up neatly on bookshelves so that they can get them out at a moment's notice when you mention, say, the Algarve, and bore you rigid with their dreary photos. Either that or they are all downloaded on to the computer so that when you say, 'Oh, what was the Algarve like?' they can email you a jpeg of them standing on the steps of their villa in the Algarve four years ago. Or (alas) they email you six of them that take an hour to download and prevent you from doing anything else, and then they send you a stupid one of them all in front of the Pyramids for their Christmas round robin, printed out on an annoying bit of A4 paper that won't stand up on any surface and keeps doing the splits and pushing all the other more conventional Christmas cards over.

What chance have I got of sorting out the holiday snaps? I mean, I come back from holiday, reverse the car up to the washing machine (as you do) and struggle to restore some sort of order for Monday morning. And I do what all normal people do with holiday snaps, I bung them in a big trunk (getting bigger every year) in the hope that one rainy day, when I have a minute, I will sort them all out. At the rate I am going, I think it'll be when all the kids have left home, when I've retrained as a florist and started early onset Alzheimers, and by then I will have forgotten where we went anyway.

I am not alone. Whenever I talk to a group of mothers the conversation always gets around to the pile of stuff we have to do. We all get out our sad little lists, our domestic reminders, our birthday card lists, our Christmas lists, and even the kitchen calendar that has everyone's movements noted on it – which we, and only we, have our heads around.

If only we could just let go. If only we could say to ourselves, 'Look, the kitchen is going to be in a muddle for the foreseeable future. The violin stand and the PlayStation mess will always be on the living room floor, so chill.' Oh, how I so wish I could take my own advice.

And with the lists come bags. Life is one long succession of bags – swimming bags, work bags, charity shop bags … Every time you go out of the front door you've got at least one bag with you. You go to work with a bag of things you need to take back to M&S in your lunch hour; you come home with a bag of supermarket stuff to make tea; the boot of your car is occupied by a judo kit bag full of things that need washing, ironing and sorting; and the dry-cleaning bag has got to be brought home.

Every time you see a woman in the street she has a bag: hand-bag, carrier bag, workbag, laptop bag. There is no end to it. Every time you get home the car has to be unloaded, then loaded again for tomorrow's bag run. Teenage Daughter leaves the house with a 'bag' the size of a pocket diary and seems to get by, while I lug around so much stuff that I've graduated to a wheelie. Just on a day-to-day basis – not for going away or anything – just for going to and from work, every day.

So all this stress, which apparently means that working mothers are now more likely than men have a heart attack before they are 50, is because we had the choice to have a career *and* run the house and family. You don't know what to do for the best. If you go out to work, you barely have time to empty your bladder; and if you're a stay-at-home mum, you have a wretched time – people treat you like pond life. All those things that fill your life, and that make life so much pleasanter for your nearest and dearest, are considered at best dull, and at worst demeaning. Whatever you do, you can't win.

HOME OR AWAY

Sadly, mothers have now divided into two distinct camps.

What happens is that women, who should really in an ideal world stick together, are divided into two camps, and reserve their most toxic venom for each other. Working mothers despise stay-at-home mothers, who they think are sad, bovine, wet, pathetic, amoeba-like creatures, and women who stay at home with their children despise working mothers as the devil – abandoning their children in order to wear a nice pair of heels and make a buck. And it's nonsense. It's ludicrous. The two should be supporting one another, but in fact they hate each other with a passion.

India Knight

You can tell which children have stay-at-home mothers and which have career mothers at a glance.

STAY-AT-HOME MOTHER	CAREER MOTHER
• Packed lunch with home-baked high-fibre scones	• Tuna mayonnaise sandwich from the petrol station
• Hair in a French knot	• Pony tail in an elastic band
• Start-rite shoes well polished	• Trainers that need a wash
• Harvest festival hamper with bouffant bows and organic produce	• Tinned baked beans and peaches, plus a banana in a plastic bag
• Gym bag neatly ironed	• Sainsbury carrier bag left at home or with rancid socks that haven't been home all term
• Breakfast of organic toast, honey and freshly squeezed orange juice	• Piece of toast in the car on the way to school
• Home-made nativity costume with custom-made wings	• Kingly robe made from a dressing gown pinned up with safety pins, with an unironed tea towel headdress.
• School holidays spent cutting and sticking, and doing creative work with clay	• Sky TV
• Handwritten and newsy thank-you letters with nicely drawn pictures	• Computerised round robin
• School projects researched and bound in stunning folder	• The dog has had it
• Children leave home at 18 and don't give their mother a second glance	• Children leave home at 18 and don't give their mother a second glance

All this apparent inadequacy means that career mums cling together, in a constant state of guilt and anxiety. And, of course, once children can express themselves, they know exactly where your Achilles heel is. 'Your job is ruining my life,' they say, or 'Why can't you come and help out in class like David's mother does?' 'Why can't you do the costumes for the play?' 'Will you be there when I get home?'

Equally, if you don't go out to work, your children are likely to ask you why you don't have a job, or what you do all day, often followed by what can only be described as a tirade from you – a blow-by-blow account of the tasks that the stay-at-home mother has to do in any one day.

THE NINE TO FIVE

So why go out to work? Most of us don't have a choice any more. A spot of light housework, and a quick change into something sex kittenish for when the husband gets home is not really an option. Once we were properly liberated, we had to go to work to earn real money (not pin money) to pay the mortgage or fund the children in university. Plus we like buying handbags a lot.

In time you come to terms with the fact that this is your lot – that working motherhood is a bad hand, so you might as well just live with it. The kids are getting a bit older and you think you'll stick it out because you have to pay for them to go to university, and they have mobiles and Sky TV to pay for. And anyway, who wants to spend the day pushing the vacuum cleaner round the house when there's no longer anyone under 12 doing Playdoh or reading story books.

But I wonder to what extent women are really built for modern working life, for the stresses and strains of office politics. We're built for the work – no question of that – built to keep going and never give in, to solve problems and to roll up our sleeves when stuff needs doing. That's what makes us so successful, so indispensable, but we end up doing two jobs; even if we don't have kids, we end up with two sets of responsibilities. And that's truly hard sometimes.

We just have to get on with it all, even though being at work is perhaps not as exciting as it once was. And 'here's the thing' (as everyone says in the office now that they all sound and behave like Simon Cowell): being at work when you're over 40 means you are already considered to be over the hill. Not just at the top of the hill with a good all-round view of things, but way down the other side. But the good thing, the really good thing, about being one of the older people in the office, if it weren't entirely naff to say so, is that, you've 'been there, done that'. You have. When they all talk about brainstorming some new ideas, you know that it is going to lead nowhere at all, but it will get you away from your desk for a day, and might involve some nice croissants or lunch. You chuck in a few ideas that you chucked into a similar brainstorming arranged three bosses ago – at a slightly poncier hotel. Not that you can crow about this, obviously. You must at all times avoid telling anyone that you tried their idea and it didn't work. It'll just make you look sad and old, and slightly bitter, so instead feign enthusiastic support and just watch it all collapse. Especially if the idea comes from one of the young things who flick their hair back constantly and think they know it all.

Having been at work for what seems like an eternity, the initial rush of enthusiasm has passed. You no longer rush headlong like a springer spaniel puppy into great rafts of work without wondering what the point is. But for all potential employers who are now crossing me off their employment list, I would like to point out that this cynicism (scepticism, should we say?), is outweighed in large dollops by the fact that I have so very much more experience. When their dignity will allow, some of the young things at work form a quiet but orderly queue at my desk to ask advice, sound me out or pick my brains, which is code for 'help' – so there, nur.

For the trainee Grumpy Old Women (or men) among you readers, there are some universal truths we have picked up during our (long) working lives that are worth sharing.

BOSSES

The trouble with bosses, or line managers, as we now call them, is that they are never there when you want them, and invariably there when you don't. They have a knack of never taking a problem off you, but instead give it back with even more work attached to it, then stand aside as if they have just solved it for you and you were an idiot to ask for help in the first place. Bosses glaze over at the details of a problem, which is exactly the bit you want them to help with. Bosses listen but don't make notes. *You* seem to be sitting there with a sad little list of things to raise with them, and they pontificate about irrelevant things they've told you before, then say they have to rush out to lunch.

You'd think that women bosses might be a godsend. Not at all. If they are childless, they have no idea, nor are they even slightly interested in, the domestic conflict you are experiencing and how difficult it is to be pulled in two different directions. On the other hand if they have children of their own then they are going to delegate work to you in buckets and bog off home early during half-term while you are still at the office.

The corporate world is organised so that the CEO's desk is empty – a shining expanse – because he doesn't do anything. Read my lips. He sits there making decisions, while everybody else scurries about and enacts them for him.

Germaine Greer

Generally bosses are older than you, but I currently have one who looks about 14 and dresses for the beach. Bosses love to sign things, which doesn't mean they actually read much. In fact, they don't bother reading anything except your expenses and the office phone bill, which they examine in microscopic detail.

It's important always to look busy. Have a screen full of something you can click on in a hurry when someone comes past and you are doing the Tesco shop or sussing out EasyJet flights or doing your returns to Boden.

Obviously, you can't go home before your boss, which makes the seats that are not in his or her full view at a premium. By the way, if you are the boss, you need to realise that you go home at 6.05 and everyone else leaves at 6.06, making sure that your car has cleared the car park first.

MEETINGS

Oh – my – God. Why do people have to arrange meetings every five minutes? They are generally a waste of time, last far too long and are really about mutual stroking, not about the matter in hand at all. Someone does a showy-off thing at the beginning, like a little dog marking its territory, then someone else gets some charts out or does the power point thing and you all stifle yawns. The only time meetings are fun is when your boss's boss turns up – then the floor-show is worth all the effort.

The first thing about meetings is that the subject matter is the easy bit; you spend only .00005 per cent of your preparation time thinking about the content, or what the problem might be, or what stats you need to bring along. Which is why most of them could be done on the phone. Meetings are about scoring goals, or not letting them in. The first thing is where to sit. Don't sit down until you know where the boss is going to sit, then don't sit *next* to them or doodle love notes on their pad. If you are sitting right next to them when they start the meeting, you are in a very vulnerable position. They might ask you out of the blue what you think of the report, and then you'll actually have to say what you think without knowing what *they* think. Which is unthinkable. Obviously, it's nothing to do with what you really think, but about getting the answer right. Either that or the boss will come to you last and then you'll look like a total prat when everyone else has scored all the obvious goals and you're left saying something dumb like, 'I think everyone has already covered all the points that I was going to make.'

Work in general has become more annoying as I've got older. Not only have dozens of less talented people overtaken me, but the whole business of work seems to have gone 'Stateside'. We all talk as if we are in some multinational boardroom in Texas when we might, in fact, be head of accounts on an industrial estate in Stourbridge.

You will be able to think of lots of other irritating phrases that people now use at work, but here are a few to get you started.

STATESPEAK	GRUMPY TRANSLATION
• Watercooler moment	• Code for 'memorable'
• Interface	• What's wrong with meet?
• Take a view	• Code for 'dump the work on someone else'
• No brainer	• People with no brains use it
• Way to go	• What do they mean, some improvement needed?
• Level playing field	• Oh, honestly …

• Where are you coming from?	• I come from Bournemouth, as it happens, but is it relevant?
• This moment in time	• 'Now' would do nicely
• Game plan	• Plan
• Mega bucks	• How sad is this one?
• Up to speed	• Briefed
• Heavy duty	• Difficult
• The big picture	• The thing that comes on after the Kia-Ora ads
• Macro and micro	• I thought they were chips you put in the microwave
• Expertise	• Knowledge
• Utilise	• Use
• Ball park	• So 80s
• In the loop	• Knowing something
• Out of the loop	• Sounds like something out of *Playschool*
• Heads up	• To summarise the main points, but to sound oh so much more trendy

So having it all, for my generation at least, seems destined to leave all of us – both the haves and the have-nots – unhappy, wondering whether the option we didn't choose might have made us happier, calmer and more fulfilled. Perhaps it is another example of too much choice making life more complicated and not necessarily more happy. Some days I wouldn't change my job for the world; other days I could happily walk away from my desk and not give a hoot about the financial fall-out. In the meantime, perhaps we Grumpy Old Women should try to be a bit more forgiving to the women on the other side of the fence.

CHAPTER THREE

Grumpy Old Men

WHAT A LOT OF FUSS AND BOTHER men have made about how grumpy they are. What have they got to be grumpy about? Some eyebrows that are going a bit Denis Healey, a spot of nasal hair and some frustrations at B&Q. Scary. We'll give them grumpy.

There we all were, loving it up at Woodstock, singing along to Cat Stevens and Fairport Convention with flowers in our hair – it was all going to be different for our generation. We were going to break free, cut the apron strings that kept our mothers busy at the kitchen sink. We were going to have the time of our lives, all our lives. We were going to do more important things than the washing and ironing. Men encouraged us to seek highly paid and stressful jobs, applauded our successful careers, and we got equal. But something went wrong. No one really explained to men that once we got further up the food chain, we would need *them* to be mothers and housewives too. But just as we are wired for neat kitchens and clean bathrooms, they are wired for not noticing one way or the other, so it feels like we're a bit stuck.

For men, things haven't changed much since they shared flats with us at university and didn't involve themselves in the washing or cleaning. If we girls thought the place needed tidying up, then we could do it; if we thought the bath needed cleaning, we could make rotas with the men's names on till we were blue in the face. They weren't really fussed whether it was that clean or not, so if we wanted it clean, then we could clean it. Now, 30 years on, they still have no concept of wiping work surfaces. If you send them to the supermarket with a shopping list nicely written out in the order they will hit the aisles, they either forget it, or buy some stupid extra items you didn't ask for, such as chilli pepper washing-up liquid, frozen chips and gravy dinners for one, or pepperoni dip that's about to go off in the bargain section – awful stuff like that. Either that or they'll spend an extra half hour choosing all the rotten tomatoes so that you won't send them again. They think we don't know that trick. They must think we were born yesterday. We changed, but how come we expected them to change too? It just didn't happen. Yes, they do stuff around the house their fathers didn't do, but only eventually.

You say, 'Will you do this?' and a chap says, 'Yes, I will.' You then say, 'When will you do it?' He says, 'I'll do it tomorrow.' So tomorrow comes and it's wearing on, and on, and on and they still haven't done it. You say, 'Are you going to do that by the end of the day?' They say, 'Yes, I'm going to do it.' But they don't do it. So you have to ask them again. If you don't ask, they forget. If you do ask, you're nagging.

Michele Hanson

In fact, while we're at it, let's just get off our chests some of the things that Grumpy Old Men do around the house that really get on our wick.

You ask them to make the bed, and when they do get around to it they vaguely and half-heartedly pull the duvet up in the direction of the pillow, then walk out of the bedroom and get on with their lives. They don't *do* plumping pillows, straightening bedspreads, or placing scatter cushions. And they haven't even *noticed* the curtain tie-backs. Trying to explain to a man how beds really need to be made is like explaining the offside rule to a woman. They just don't get it. Don't really *want* to get it. A marriage counsellor told me of a couple who had sorted out all their deep emotional problems except the biggest outstanding issue, which was making the bed. This was impossible to compromise on, so they had to have one day with her bed-making standards, and one day with his, presumably for the rest of their lives. I tell you this just to demonstrate that these things are important to us.

Men's idea of wiping the work surfaces down (when asked) is just to wipe all the mess on to the floor. Dustpan and brush? No chance. When they wash up they plunge the cafetière into the washing-up bowl without emptying it, so coffee grounds swish around and go over everything else, including the dishcloth (which you bleached the night before, just as Kim and Aggie do). As far as my Grumpy Old Man is concerned, the kitchen sink is an alternative to the bin. In fact, his knowledge of household cleaning has not moved on since he was sharing a flat at university with four other blokes and they had the one J-cloth between them for the whole three years, without ever washing it, of course. The fine detail of glass wipes, floor wash and Cif mousse are of no interest whatsoever.

If I ask my Grumpy to peg washing out, he does it so that it dries with more creases than when he pulled it out of the machine, and when you tell him nicely, carefully, diplomatically (on a good day anyway) how to do it better next time, he looks uninterested, distracted, like a naughty child being told off who doesn't care. I feel like saying, 'Look at me when I'm talking to you,' but for some reason I think he might just tell me to bog off and 'do it yourself, then'.

Even in the garden he makes a mess and doesn't clear it up. He weeds a border and just leaves all the weeds and stuff in piles on the lawn instead of bagging it up, saying the wind will soon blow it all away. He cut a tree down three August bank holidays ago and it still lies where it fell. I think he spent about ten minutes trying to ignite it and to make a bonfire, then lost interest and went back into the house to listen to the sports report.

If he irons a shirt, it takes him about 90 minutes, and then he realises he hasn't turned the iron on, or he leaves the ironing board in the living room for days. Mugs are scattered all over the house and garden where he leaves them. I then go and collect them, put them in the dishwasher and get them all into neat matching rows in the kitchen cupboards to make me feel like I have some control over all the muddle again.

It's not that he is wilfully lazy, or that he is wilfully difficult, it's just that – well, he doesn't really think any of it matters much. So in the end, if I want the kitchen floor cleaned the way I like it cleaned, then I have to do it myself. I wish I could be indifferent to the mess and muddle; I'd be calmer and probably a touch happier.

We manage, though, as best we can. But then men cleverly claim that women are so much better than they are at multi-tasking, so we end up writing a bestselling novel on the way to work and defrosting the freezer while ironing shirts, and they have neatly sidestepped organising the school pick-ups, bagging up the school dinner money and doing the fish-finger run. It's not that they actually refuse to do anything – they are smarter than that. They say they'll do it 'later', or they'll do it 'soon', or they'll do it 'tomorrow'. That way you can't cross it off your list. You keep having to check when they *are* going to do it, and keep reminding them, which they call nagging. You can't win.

DRIVING US MAD

It's not just at home that men are annoying. They are also
pretty inept on the road … they still haven't got the hang of
clutch control, jerking you forwards and backwards when you
come up to junctions. They also take roundabouts far too fast
so that you end up leaning over like some outrider on a
motorbike, and they have no idea how long it takes to stop.
I wish the brake on my side would work better. I press it
ostentatiously and he takes no notice whatsoever, which is
infuriating. And then they have the cheek to criticise our driving.
I rather *like* the middle lane on the motorway. I sit in it for
hundreds of miles on end, listening to the radio, daydreaming,
checking my lipstick, and am quite happy watching dozens of
male drivers going past and doing wanker signs at me.
Marvellous. I daydream a lot when I'm driving. I wonder about
those huge trucks with photos of cherry Bakewell tarts on the
side – can they be full of just Bakewell tarts? If not, what else
is in there? How do they work out who needs the most cherry
Bakewells? Then I start getting cross about all the CO_2 emitted
in the cause of delivering these bleeding Bakewell tarts that are
only going to make us fatter anyway. What happened to the
railways? Can't they take all the freight instead of it clogging up
our motorways? And every time I overtake one of these vast
trucks the length of a football pitch I assume they are going to
pull out and crush me against the barrier because they couldn't
be arsed to indicate. If I see one of the drivers on the phone
I wave my fist at him. I got so mad about one of them that
I called the police to complain but when I got through the
policeman asked me whether I was calling on my mobile
phone, and of course I was, so that got a bit embarrassing.

When my mother learnt to drive it was quite a big deal.
There were jokes on the telly about lady drivers, stickers about

lady drivers that you bought on holiday in Weston-super-Mare to put in your Ford Anglia, and cartoons in the *Daily Express*. Everyone thought women drivers were a bit of a craze – they'd never last, I mean, really. Unfortunately, my mother did do her bit to perpetuate this prejudice: she could only ever drive on ordinary roads because she found dual carriageways and motorways far too frightening. She once took the slip road to Warwick by mistake and found herself on the feeder road to the M1 – my father had to go and get her.

Then there's the directions thing. Men will not ask for help, will they? I send Grumpy to get some fresh custard and he's away for hours and hours and hours … And when I call him on the mobile he says he's looked everywhere for the custard and he can't find it. 'Well, just bloody well ask someone, for God's sake.' I go into a shop and simply skid up to someone and ask them to find what I want, no messing. But not him. So asking for directions is the same – as you might expect. My problem is that I ask for directions and then don't understand the answer, but pretend I do, or I presume Grumpy Old Man is listening to the answer and taking it all in for me, so then we set off again and are none the wiser.

In some ways you have to feel a little bit sorry for men of a certain age. They use words like 'cool' or 'wild' and believe that people think they are both those things. But we know better. We know they are still wearing Y-fronts and turning them inside out on day two. We know they spill their soup down their front, they fall asleep in front of the telly and listen to James Alexander Gordon in the bath every Saturday at 5 p.m. for the football results, probably with a baseball cap on.

Middle-aged men are fine if they accept that they're middle-aged men. In fact, they're rather interesting when they accept that they're middle-aged men. But when they decide that they're going to act as if they're 19 or 20, and dress in a style that is appropriate to that age, then it really is pathetic. It's even more pathetic than a woman dressed up 20 years too young.

Ann Widdecombe

We know they have a Wayne Fontana vinyl collection in the spare room – that they've had time to sort out alphabetically. They do try. They have learnt one or two things over the years. They know that when we ask 'how do I look?' it is important to get the answer right. It's no longer good enough just mumbling 'fine'. My husband does now know at least to *look* at me before answering, and his idea of a thumbs-up is 'smart', which is not quite what I had in mind. I'd have preferred 'ravishing' or 'irresistible', but there we are. You have to be grateful.

Men don't have it that easy, of course. At least women get some time off when they have kids. We get a break from the nine to five routine, but men have to trudge on to the bitter end to pay for the university fees, and watch other men and women overtake them at work. They come home to chaos and, unlike their fathers, get thrown a nasty lasagne to put in the microwave for supper. I imagine they all wish they had wives like Katie in the Oxo ads, or someone who would lovingly make their bed and iron their shirts for them.

And they do get themselves in a state. They get so petty and wound up about people touching their car, or moving their comb. They buy an air rifle to shoot at the squirrels in the garden who ruin their beloved vegetable plot. I've noticed that my Grumpy Old Man is increasingly preoccupied with killing or maiming pests, most recently wasps in a jam jar and water trap he has put on the bird table. First thing he does when he comes home from work is to check how many he has nuked since breakfast. 'Sixteen!' he shouts triumphantly up the stairs, as if any of us are the slightest bit interested. 'Fifty-four just since Saturday,' he exclaims. Which means he has counted all the corpses … Tragic or what? It's the equivalent of a little boy jumping on a beetle and squashing it to death. He's even got one of those blowtorch weedkiller devices that he sent off for, which means he wanders round the patio and garden with the flame-thrower on full blast. If they sold weapons of mass destruction at the ironmonger's, he'd buy some and they would keep him busy and amused till his dying day – and other people's, probably. It's starting to happen with security – more and more padlocks, bolts and security devices on the garden shed, the garage and the back door to keep everyone away from his prized possessions. Annoying notes everywhere about where the window keys are in case of fire. He even talked about having a fire drill the other day. I thought *I* was a nervous wreck.

WEAR AND TEAR

What is super-infuriating is that men tend to age better than we do. People say they look distinguished when they start to go grey, and unless they do something really dumb, such as dye their hair and eyebrows jet-black, they usually manage to retain their pulling power. In fact, men who are fat, 50 and suddenly on the market because they are widowed or divorced usually attract a *queue* of single women within days.

In my next life I'm going to come back as a rather good-looking, even quite fat and plain 50-year-old man, who's just been widowed or sadly divorced, and I would go to the country and I would clean up. I would get a bonk every night of the week.

Jilly Cooper

Which is a bit much considering their appalling dress sense. For some reason, middle-aged men think they look good in trainers and baseball caps. Why haven't they twigged that they look good in nicely tailored suits, instead of wearing children's clothes, and what's with the pedal-pusher look? It looks good on my 12-year-old, but not on Peter Mandelson. Either they dress like children or they get it all wrong and wear a shirt and tie with their beloved jeans. Not a good look. And on the dance floor they are particularly embarrassing. 'Brown Sugar' comes on and menopausal man starts prancing around doing silly air-punching Mick Jagger impressions. And they think they look so good. They do not look good. The hair thing is a bit depressing for them though, which obviously explains their baseball cap obsession.

Then there's the snoring. That's no joke. He settles down to watch the telly and it starts.

I swear there are drugs in the upholstery of his chair. Because honestly he just gets near the television and goes zzzz ... It's known as the drugged chair.

Dillie Keane

Physically they age in a slightly more mellow way than women. Physically possibly, but at the same time it's not women who fall asleep in the middle of television programmes for no apparent reason. In the middle of conversations actually, or is that just me? One minute there's an adult person you're engaging with on some vaguely cerebral level, and the next minute there's somebody quietly snoring. That must be a sort of genetic thing, because women don't do that.

Kathryn Flett

Quietly snoring ... lucky Kathryn. I wake up at 2 a.m. and he's off. Sometimes I move beds three times a night. I try to roll him over, build a pillow dam which props him up on his side, and he still finds a way of rolling back. I could take the carving knife to him some nights, and if they heard the volume and

sheer awfulness of it, no one would think the worse of me. He
wakes himself up with it sometimes; the kids can hear him
down the landing. He hits the pillow and he's asleep instantly.
There is nothing more annoying when you're up with a hot
flush and thinking about how you're going to have time to get
some king prawns by Friday evening than the person next to
you making a noise as loud as the hedge trimmer, as if they're
saying, 'I'm asleep and you're not.' Then he wakes up and says
he didn't have a very good night. Hello?

DOING IT

No wonder our children assume we don't do it any more.
The very idea would be bound to make them gag. The trouble
with middle-aged men is that they seem to go off sex big time,
but menopause gives Grumpy Old Women a sudden and
unhealthy interest in sex. I start looking at couples wondering
when they last did IT in the way that I used to when I was 16.
It's getting rather unhealthy. I run around the place, front
bottom ablaze, with no one but Grumpy to help me out. It's a
bad combination. God knows what would happen if I took
some Viagra. I'd be sitting on the tumble-drier all day.

CHAPTER FOUR

Stuck in the middle

IF YOU'VE GOT THIS FAR, you will realise that I, as self-appointed form captain of Grumpy Old Women everywhere, feel that for all sorts of reasons we are getting a rough deal in life. Having done some serious scientific research on the matter (as in, sitting in the bath thinking about it with a mug of Earl Grey), I think this is partly because we don't really feel we fit in anywhere any more. We're at a sort of in-between stage. The very term 'middle-aged' implies a sort of in-between, nowhere arrangement. If we went into Tammy Girl, the shop assistants would send for the SAS to get us off the premises sharpish. On the other hand if we turned up at the village hall for the afternoon 'Whist Drive for the Young at Heart', people would assume we had come to help rather than join in. Although this may be, to an extent, wishful thinking, I feel our role is to facilitate things for the generations above and below us, rather than to facilitate much for ourselves. We're at everyone else's beck and call.

For instance, if you go to a wedding, you're not young enough to lark about on the bouncy castle or get drunk with the teenagers. Instead, you get stuck with some dreary woman called Brenda going on about her creative writing class. Worse than that, if you do try to talk to some young people, say, in their 20s or 30s, they recoil in disgust. You could spend the entire evening telling them your funniest stories and most fascinating anecdotes, and they would still be looking over your shoulder for someone younger to talk to because to the rest of the world you are a boring old bag. If only they knew how remarkable, how fantastic, how funny, how sexy we all really are.

Young people get up your nose, but then again, old people irritate the hell out of you too. In short, it seems like Grumpy Old Women are stuck in the middle, sandwiched miserably between the two other generations.

No one will be surprised to hear that *young* people irritate the hell out of me. It's the law for the over-40s to loathe and detest young people, or 'young people today', as we now need to call them, but this generation takes the biscuit. They are, surely, infinitely more irritating than we were at their age? They stand around gormlessly and aimlessly in a state of inertia while we get on with all the dreary tasks that need doing, such as filling the car with unleaded, taking the wheelie bin out for the dustmen, and queuing at the dry cleaners. Young people wear disgustingly revealing clothes that show off their midriff, their cleavage and their God-awful tattoos, they wear ridiculous jeans with slashes in that look as if they have been swimming with sharks, and those ridicoulously impractical baggy jeans that scuff the ground. They're either plugged into their mini-disk, programming their iPod or playing with their dance mat. What happened to good old-fashioned going out on your bike, or a nice healthy game of tag? They obviously need a big dose of fresh air, so in the holidays I rush about like an enthusiastic puppy, suggesting picnics and barbecues – all sorts of outdoor adventures that will make me think that I am in one of the Famous Five books, reliving my own childhood, with treasure to find and ginger snaps to put in my trunk, and they all look at me as if I'm mad, and want to go to the cinema or go shopping with their friends.

They all need to go to Brownies and learn how to do reef knots, or go camping with Arkala and Brown Owl and be made to sit in a wet circle round a dwindling bonfire. Or spend an entire evening in a draughty village hall with Brown Owl blowing on a whistle and making you run from one side of the hall to the other according to whether she shouts 'port' or 'starboard'. They then go home for some beans on toast in front of *Crossroads*. This is code for getting our own back, making us feel better about the fact that they are all having a carefree time making whoopee and we are hoovering under the settee.

Either they are lolling about making a mess or throwing litter, or they are standing around in those Gap tops with

hoods on, looking all menacing and frightening, or sticking their chewing gum under the table at McDonald's and generally being a bloody nuisance.

I would make hoods illegal. All these young boys today, they think they're hard because they've got their hood up. Well, it wouldn't take much, a little bit of government legislation, to cut all the hoods out of every single piece of clothing. We know why you've got your hoods up – when you go into that shop you think, 'Oh, there's a security camera. I'll put my hood up.' Well, in future no hoods, hoods off!
Jenny Eclair

Then there's all their binge drinking and trips to Ibiza, where they apparently shag on the beach quite openly for every poor sod to see, throw up, show off their love bites and don't wear nearly enough clothes. It's no wonder we enjoy seeing them suffer – the plasters on their heels where their absurd pointy high heels have given them blisters, their horrid nose piercings that will look so absurd when they are in the Derby and Joans. Maybe there should be an ad campaign warning young people that if they don't try very hard at anything they'll be given a job emptying all the dog-poo bins around the country. That'd give them something to aim for. Or not aim for, more to the point.

And what happened to morals – to use a very old-fashioned word. Why don't young people give up their seat on the bus? Why do they swear at us and call us old bags if we so much as dare to tell them to pick up their litter or stop vandalising someone's car? They have turned us into a cliché of ourselves.

The worst thing you can do with young people is say, 'Yeah, when I was your age … ' because they just hate you instantly for saying that. You were never their age; their age is unique; they are the first people to ever have been young, and the experience they are going

through is unique … much more profound and resonant than
anything you could have gone through, so never ever try to connect
with young people.

Kathryn Flett

But instead of idiotic suggestions, such as bringing back the
three Rs or compulsory spells in the army, it would be more
sensible if young people could be made to do all the dreary
stuff we have to do every day leaving us free to write in to
Radio 2 and check our lottery tickets. Either that, or we
should be allowed to give them one big, long collective telling-
off, with no butting in, no hair flicking and no answering back.
We could really give them a piece of our mind.

Then there's all their dire music. Justin Timberlake,
Christina Aguilera – see, I know the names at least – pointing
at their willies or pushing their front bottoms in our faces,
wearing just their knickers on stage, writhing about for all to
see. I mean, what does that say about our own youth? A spot
of ping-pong in the local church youth club, some snogging
behind the bike sheds if you were lucky … and our music was
just, well, so much classier. I'm not talking Acker Bilk or
anything stupid; but the Shadows, they had real style, real
presence, with their crossover walk thing. My kids listen to
today's sexist drivel – rasta rappy stuff that seems to be all
about girls being juicy and getting laid, and all sorts of things
that I find very offensive – and, now that I have two teenage
daughters, it makes me blush. That stuff makes me fear for
them, makes me feel sexual liberation has taken us backwards
not forwards.

It's not even as if you can sit them down and impart some
sound advice. Once you start trying to tell them that you were
young once, and yes – amazingly – you also went through a
rebellious stage, they just start rolling their eyes and looking as

if they might be sick. The fact that you were once a hip young thing with a pair of purple loons and a copy of *Oz*, you smoked a bit of dope and went to all-night parties, is irrelevant, invisible, implausible. The person that stands before them is a middle-aged podgy woman with a crap outfit on and a pair of comfy shoes. What the hell would she know? About anything.

Still, there are compensations: we have more money than the young, they have to do exams and we don't – unless we are mad enough to join the Open University (although I do hear their study weekends involve a good deal of dorm-hopping and hanky-panky) – and they have a boring Saturday job, such as stacking the shelves in the local supermarket, serving behind the baker's counter, or working in B&Q when someone like us comes in to make trouble. Yeeha! They never ever know the price of anything they're selling. We ask them how much it costs and they say, 'Isn't it written on it?' Gosh, hadn't thought of that! And they invariably have to go and ask someone older and wiser. Back of the net!

I love it in shops when I make them do some mental arithmetic, which they find impossible. If I'm in the butcher's and the total comes to £10.86, I offer them some change with my £20 note and ask whether the odd 20p helps, so that they have to try to work out the sum in their head instead of just keying it all into the automatic till. That gets them in a real flummox and they go all hot and red in the face and say, 'No, no, it's fine', even if they need the change. In fact, if you ask them anything at all, such as, 'Does this stain remover work on carpets?' they look gormless as usual, and start reading out the label. Dur. I think I might have been able to work that one out. Or if you ask for something in a size 16, they say, 'Isn't there one out?' 'Well, *you* tell me,' is what I say. Don't just stand there by the changing rooms looking ridiculous in your skinny-winny top showing your belly button and thinking about who you are going to snog on Saturday night. Get your arse over here and give me some service.

The wicked truth is that although we might not be able to dress in skinny little ra-ra skirts or flirt with men under thirty without looking like a total saddo, we might be able – if we put our minds to it, complained a lot and really let rip – to get them the sack.

Of course, they all have so very much more time than we do – hours and hours and hours of doing I know not what in their bedrooms, hours of changing their ring tones, or texting their friends or going into chat rooms. I've never been in a chat room. They called them coffee bars in my day. And then you ask them to help you fold up the ironing and there's a lot of huffing and puffing. Bob a Job week, that's what we did. So there.

The best thing to do is just treat young people as an alien species, which is what they are, and between the ages of about 12, 13 to 20, 21, just ignore them.

Kathryn Flett

Trouble is, you can't just ignore them. Irritatingly, we do need them to get us on to the Net to do the shopping, to help us programme our videos and stuff. For that kind of thing, they do have their uses.

GIRLY TROUBLE

Young people in general are very, very trying indeed, but teenage girls are something else. A species on their own. Nice of God to plan things so that just as our teenage daughters are hitting puberty, we are also at our hormonal worst. They save their special attitude problems for their mothers. There is only so much door slamming a house can take.

And they're so full of themselves, with their perfect teeth and straightened hair and being all full-on and self-confident. How did that happen? When I was their age I was racked with self-doubt and embarrassment, but these girls don't give a monkey's, so what hope have we got of being able to control and influence them?

They fit a doorbell to their bedroom and when you ring it they spend ages coming to the door and then snarl, 'What?' If you tell them off, they get all huffy and puffy and hurt, and use one of their favourite words, which is 'sorree'. And they have worked out that the best way to keep all information from you at all times is never to talk to you, in fact, never really to form words properly. So you ask them if they'd like some lunch and they say something like, 'Ah,' which isn't yes and isn't no and isn't even I don't know – it's just a noise.

They spend hours toning their skin and filing their nails while we are loading the dishwasher, and then they emerge looking like Jennifer Aniston and we emerge like Judith Chalmers on a bad day. Then, if we go on holiday with them, we have to lie on a sunbed next to them. Thank God for sarongs.

They spend their entire free time (which is *most* of the time) watching *Friends* or *Will and Grace*, and consequently talk as if they are in an episode themselves. They use the word 'like' three times in every sentence: 'I thought they would *like* go with the *like* trousers. You said you would *like* pay for the *like* cinema. I do *like* want to but I can't. I have *like* tidied my room but it got *like* untidy again.'

Smack. Imagine being their English teacher.

They flick their hair around and throw their heads back a lot. They read your *Heat* magazine, use your nail varnish and generally mess up the bathroom big time. They steal the phone from the kitchen and spend an hour talking to one of their mates that they've been at school with all day. Then they leave the phone in their room, so when it rings everyone else has to go hunting for it.

And then they have the cheek to be so snooty about anything you do. 'Shall we get an Indian?' you say one Friday night when you're feeling a bit flush. 'God, it's so, like, rubbish there. Can't we go to … ' naming another establishment that's really expensive. You suggest they buy their underwear from M&S and they are aghast – no thanks. Has to be La Senza at least. 'No, I don't want that perfume. Is it Armani?' Actually, I blame the Osbornes. How come Sharon manages to be so damn patient with the two of them? It's making our teenagers worse than they need to be, I swear.

And they turn me into my mother. I say things to them like my mother used to say to me: 'You're not going out like that are you? You look common,' I say, or worse, 'You look tarty.' It's all so depressing, and all so inevitable.

OLD GIRL TROUBLE

Then, on the other side of this sandwich we're squashed in the middle of, are old people – really old people. Of course the main reason we find *them* so bloody irritating is because we are heading in the same direction faster than we would like to admit. It's not just my body that is turning into my mother's. My brain is going all fuzzy around the edges too, like hers. I'm not as bad as her, but I'm pretty bad. I've bought Auntie Doreen the same Christmas present three years running because each time it seemed such a brilliant idea; people answer the phone and I forget who I've dialled or why I've rung in the first place; and I have Post-It notes everywhere because otherwise I forget everything.

I've not yet got to my mother's stage of writing down my four most important telephone numbers on the back of a piece of cornflake packet and putting them in my handbag for handy reference. She even has one that says ME – with her own mobile number in case she forgets. Trouble is, you get to her age and you have to be on your guard. One day a social worker with a short hairdo and dangly earrings will pounce on you and ask you the name of the prime minister and what day it is. Out of the blue. Say something stupid like John Major, and you've had it. You'll be carted off to a plastic winged armchair in a room smelling of cabbage at the nearest old people's home. *Aladdin* at Christmas with Peter Duncan, if you're lucky.

But old people will get in our way: they push in at the checkout, limping a bit and saying they're old and pretending they haven't noticed the queue; they go about the place chatting and chirping on the pavement, holding everyone up. Some people find them cute. Well, I assume some people find them cute. Not.

It's Christmas Eve and you're exhausted. You've got the last-minute shopping and you've been waiting for half an hour in a queue, then this old person goes by with a basketful of groceries and says, 'Oh, I'm old, can you let me pass? I have to go past because I've got to collect me pension … ' or something. And they shame you into saying, 'Oh yes, all right,' and actually I want to kill them.

Dillie Keane

They are constantly whinging on about their rights, the good old days, the war, their pensions and everything, and yet my mother seems to have about 500 per cent more leisure time than I do, and about twice as much disposable income as I do. They don't even knit any more.

And old people are obsessed with bargains. They buy those horrible cheap broken biscuits from Poundstretcher, and

they don't believe in sell-by dates, so if you go round for tea, you get some nasty bit of rancid cheese they've scraped the mould off, or some chocolates they've had in the wardrobe for nine months. I suppose when you do get old the logic is that you don't want to buy a new bed or a new car because you might not get your money's worth – you could pop your clogs any minute – so you make do; but really, they go too far!

And everything is such a lot of fuss and bother. They fuss on about trying to find the loo and make a huge mountain out of the easiest of train journeys. Their bags are full of tissues and toffees and extra strong mints. You have to write everything down for them and go and get their pension and prescriptions. You have to run them into town to meet their chums for a coffee or for lunch at the drop-in centre, while *you* run around doing more errands and *they* have a nice relaxed chat. At least when you were 12 they did *your* washing.

I have started to get into pottering, just as old people do. I spend hours and hours in my dressing gown and slippers, mooching about the house, just tidying up, collecting some margarine tubs that might come in handy, watering the plants. I've also started to get chatty with strangers at the bus stop or station, complaining about the wait and going into needlessly long explanations about things, which makes me look like I have no one to talk to at home. I'll go into a shop and say stupid things like, 'Now, I bought this a year ago, and I thought this might go with it. I was wondering if you are still doing those nice lamps with the maroon edging. No? Oh that's a pity. Well, I think I might put it in the conservatory … ' The shop girls look at me pityingly.

I talk to strangers about the weather, normally people of my own age or older, with immense interest, not because I can't think of anything else to say – *au contraire* – but because what the weather is doing is absolutely critical to me now that I am middle-aged. I watch the news with no real interest in the stories, but to see whether they have got their coats on down south as well as up in the north where I live. I watch something about Rome and think to myself, 'Why don't I live there? We've had the heating on for a month here.' I watch the seasons change with the delight of a child. I remember the nature table at infant school being full of stuff, such as horse chestnut leaves and conkers and catkins, and thinking (even at the age of six) how boring would you have to be to take an interest in that? Now I think it would be marvellous to grow a plant from a dried broad bean, or watch a horse chestnut go through its amazing processes of growing into a tree.

It's like gardening … Now there are things that annoy

the hell out of me about gardening, namely garden centres, which are like supermarkets but dearer. Also our local garden centre tends to attract the very worst of the bunch in terms of pimply youths who serve you, and who don't even know the difference between a perennial and an annual. And, if you're not careful, gardening just becomes an extension of housework. But now that I am older, I'm so much more interested in being in the garden. I remember my parents would receive people for Sunday lunch (it was before dinner parties – either that or we weren't nearly posh enough) and they'd have their ham sandwiches and fruit salad (out of a tin) and then my parents and the guests would go round the garden, which was about the size of the normal Prêt à Manger, and talk about the hydrangeas and the roses and stuff for what seemed like hours. I used to think they must be so bored, so terminally bored to talk to people about anything like that, and now, guess what?

So I'm softening to old people because I am turning into one, and I think all this aggression and sarkiness that I've got down on paper about them is really me kicking and screaming on my way into it – a sort of denial process. Soon acceptance will come, and then beige will take over, and I shall buy one of those wicker baskets posh old ladies use for shopping, and join the Women's Royal Voluntary Service.

But I think the truth is that my mother's generation was happier; they didn't have to worry about whether to go for a career or not. If they remained spinsters they probably did go for a career in insurance or MI5, otherwise they could spend their day doing impressions of Katie Boyle and Zena Skinner. They had some time to themselves, coffee mornings and *Woman's Hour*, and shopping was altogether a more social experience; you got to know the butcher and the greengrocer, and they even delivered.

Of course, by the time I reach their age the pathetic pension that I have been contributing to for 40 years will probably amount to enough to buy me a pair of tights. They'll have scrapped state pensions, I imagine, so I'll probably still be at work well into my 70s. We have so much to look forward to.

CHAPTER FIVE

Fun

FUN ... I DO VAGUELY REMEMBER IT, chatting and giggling
until the early hours, sitting in a field with some good friends
and a bottle of wine and losing track of time (losing track of
time: imagine!), taking each day as it came, waking up and
not having any plans or chores ahead. Just being carefree.
I remember all that. *Just*. It usually seemed to happen in
summer, which may account for why I am now so totally
obsessed with the weather and now hate and detest being
indoors when it is sunny. But I can't do that carefree thing any
more. All the predictable stuff gets in the way – too much to
do, too many responsibilities, the mortgage to pay, the job to
do, the children to look after, my mother to visit. But more
than that, more pernicious than that, I have a horrible feeling
that even if I were stripped of all those chores, errands and
responsibilities, I would still be unable to chill out and have an
unlimited amount of fun. I have lost the knack.

I suppose there are glimpses of fun: the end of a game
of Junior Scrabble, or the conclusion of a project at work, or,
one day in the future, seeing an item about Andrew Lloyd
Webber's latest musical being a huge flop. But the thing that
stops me having prolonged periods of carefree fun is the

anxiety that has crept up on me over the years, which is now so well bedded in that I can't go about the simplest of tasks without catastrophising what might happen. There is simply too much to worry about – all the time. I have seen too many episodes of *999* and *Casualty*.

I can't just stroll down a coastal path by the sea and soak up the general wonderfulness of it all. I am constantly on my guard in case someone slips and tumbles to their death, because I remember the *999* episode where someone fell on to the rocks in Cornwall while the tide was rising at an inch per minute, and had to cling on by their anorak while the air-sea rescue circled and other holiday-makers watched and felt good to be alive. If it happened to them, it could happen to us. 'One minute people were walking along in the sunshine, and the next it is a life or death situation,' I can hear Michael Buerk intoning, as the *999* music clangs away to make sure we know to bite our nails because it's going to be really nasty to watch.

I can't just walk nonchalantly through a farmyard with the dog without wondering whether there is an underground slurry pit like the one in *Casualty*, into which a five-year-old sank without trace, or whether a freak herd of antelope might emerge from the cowshed and push over a tractor that crushes my upper body – like the episode where the man's heart stopped beating and he had only two seconds to live before the ambulance arrived. See what I mean? If I go cycling with the kids, I can't just have fun and freewheel down the easy bits. I am on full Red Alert in case someone corners carelessly, or a truck suddenly sheds its load and crushes all three of us. If not that, then the kids get sucked into a combine harvester and thrown out of the shute thing at the back in little bite-sized pieces … See what a nightmare it is just being me?

It's not even as if I help the situation by all this worrying, and you can guarantee that if anyone does come a cropper,

it will be me. I spend my entire life constantly on my guard, mentally prepared with emergency numbers, procedures and some Savlon dry spray. The first time I flew with our youngest I took the precaution of packing her swimming armbands in the hand luggage in case we came down on water and there wasn't time to find her lifejacket. At least I didn't blow them up …

Even everyday situations are a worry. The girls go into town and I have to send them off with a little safety chat: 'Do remember to keep on the pavement. Go single file if you have to. Remember that time I nearly ran someone over? Well, remember to look right just there, as well as left at that other junction, won't you?' They're not listening. Their eyes glaze over and they think you are just mad. Bonkers. Goes in one ear and straight out of the other.

Nothing, not even a game of tag in the park, is a worry-free zone.

The stupid thing is that in an emergency I am simply the worst person to have around anyway. I go to pieces. I can't look at anyone's wound because I have been known to faint, and I am likely to just stand there, helplessly frozen with fear in the hope that the much more level-headed Grumpy Old Man that I live with will take over. The one and only time he has needed *my* help in an emergency, when his shoulder dislocated at two in the morning, the ambulance crew arrived and had to see to me first because I had passed out in sheer panic and knocked my head on the doorstep.

FUN AT THE DOCTOR'S

Then there's the chronic hypochondria. Now that the Internet is full of medical data, hypochondriacs like me are exposed to all sorts of new information, which just ratchets up the anxiety to a frenzy. There should be a way of putting a bar on people like me typing words such as 'melanoma' or 'bone cancer' into the Google search box because I scrutinise and underline all the symptoms listed in the articles that come up. Then I decide that yes, I do indeed have *it* – obviously – I've got it, have had it for weeks probably. In any one week I can have various forms of cancer – breast, skin and bowel being the most frequent – then some days I get a bit of brain cancer or the occasional superbug. I go to the doctor to get it checked out, but am now doing this so regularly that I get one of those looks that says, 'Oh, here she is again.'

When I get into the doctor's surgery she's got my file in front of her. It's a small folder, about A5, not designed to hold very much, but it is bulging to bursting point with notes, letters, charts and results of all of my imagined illnesses. I suppose that's all right if you've been a patient for the last 20 years, but we've lived here for only three years and I am only in my 40s. They've probably got some code in capitals after my name so that if a locum is unlucky enough to see me one day, he or she will know not to take me too seriously and get rid of me, or suggest I go for a particularly unpleasant test – usually with a camera and a tube in an unfortunate place – so that it delays me coming back for a little while. I wonder what the code might be: TW (Time Waster)? MWLBTAT (Menopausal Woman Likely to Burst into Tears at Any Time)? It needs to convey that I am slightly dysfunctional and should be ejected from the surgery sharpish.

Of course, while I am waiting to see the doctor about whatever killer disease I have at any one time, I've already worked out the next worry because I've been browsing one of those carousels with leaflets about other forms of cancer, or skin conditions (complete with nasty photos). So by the time I get to see the doctor I have mentally moved on, have already placed another (serious) illness and its symptoms on the backburner, ready to hold centre stage when the results of the tests on my current scare prove negative.

In between doctor's appointments I am checking daily on my symptoms of any one of about five illnesses – on the Internet, by talking to friends, and in one of the many medical dictionaries that my Grumpy Old Man tries to throw away or hide. Naturally, if I meet someone who has had the disease, or has a disease I haven't heard of, then I get that too. Then I might call NHS Direct, which is a boon for hypochondriacs like me. You can call them 24 hours a day, although I notice they have got a bit wise to this lately: they put you on to a nurse first to assess your symptoms, which is code for sorting out the drunks or the sexual perverts, or probably the serial hypochondriacs like me who just waste everyone's time. They ask you whether your breathing is all right (I assume if you say no they might put you at the top of the telephone queue to speak to an actual doctor, but I am keeping this trick in reserve in case I get one of those moles that are all dark round the outside or something that really can't wait until the next morning). So then you get through to the doctor and have a nice chat. After a while, and after quite a lot of pushing on my part, they say that it doesn't really sound like I've got *it*, but that it might be an idea to get it checked out by my own doctor some time when I have a minute. This is my ticket to the doctor's the following morning. I can go in and say that the NHS helpline said it would be a good idea for me to get it looked at, so then they have to give me an appointment.

You can imagine what I was like when the kids were small. There was always some rash to worry about, or they'd run a temperature and look a bit flushed, so I would automatically assume they had meningitis or were at death's door. I would ring the doctor and say there was a red rash (this always gets them worried and usually means the doctor come round after hours as they are afraid of being sued if it does turn out to be the big M). One of their trick questions was always, 'Is this your first baby?' And when it wasn't, they took you seriously (which in my case was usually a mistake). If it was your first child, they would write you off as an anxious mother.

When the kids were small I'd be scanning the index of Penelope Leach's childhood medicine book every five minutes, or ringing the emergency helpline for new mothers at Queen Charlotte's Hospital, the one they give you for the first few days when you get baby home. They would ask me, 'How old is baby?' and expect me to say six or seven days. I'd say, 'Well, she's three actually, but I am a bit concerned because … ' and then they'd have to listen to it all, and be nice and helpful and calm me down.

OUT TO PLAY

Fairgrounds are my worst nightmare. When the kids were really small they could go on those nice gentle fire engines on carousels and they'd be happy. I'd still have to do a quick mental risk assessment before I let them on, and I'd have a sneaky word with the ghastly man running the ride to stop it before the end because I didn't like the look of something. At Disney I was fine when we were still in the 'It's a Small World' type of rides, or Pirates of the Caribbean, and I even quite liked the lovely umbrella ride over London on the Peter Pan ride, but now the kids are older they're into Space Mountain and rides that involve being strapped in at the neck. I can't even watch.

Disney I can avoid by simply refusing to pay for holidays to go there, but the biggest, foulest, most expensive travelling funfair comes to our town once a year and I dread it. It's all sick and love bites, and now the girls are at the age where they go on the Waltzer, and the tattooed attendants spin them round more than anyone else because they are giggly girls, and the more they scream, the more they spin them round. This is my idea of a nightmare. Even when they go on the dodgems I have to keep mouthing to them to keep their arms and hands inside just in case they get bashed and crushed. I despise the men running the ride so much that I imagine they pick up body parts at the end of the evening and scrape crushed flesh off each ride before moving on and carelessly putting up the bloody thing in someone else's town. I mean, you can't tell me they're going to check it all systematically. Probably too busy shagging in those ghastly caravans, or having a new set of tattoos done. Now I'm sounding all stuck up and Hyacinth Bouquet. But then that's my prerogative.

The whole of society seems to be on a mission to scare the pants off me, off us all. It scares us into checking our breasts for lumps every other day, scares us into calling the emergency services when our child is late back from Brownies or when we see a carrier bag next to a bin in the park and assume it contains a bomb. We can't send the kids on paper rounds because they might be snatched by one of the (many) paedophiles in our neighbourhood, and we can't walk home alone at night for fear of just about anything you can think of. And if we do walk unaccompanied from the station, we do so with our house keys in our hands, ready to put them straight in the door in case we are being followed, or in case we are bundled into a serial killer's car. We cross the road if we see anyone we don't like the look of, which is everyone except nice old ladies because, apart from anything else, they are likely to be mugged first. We buy padlocks and alarms and personal security devices, we carry around nasty aerosol sprays to squirt directly into the eyes of anyone who dares to attack us (like we'd have it to hand, and like we'd not end up with it in our own eyes instead!).

I can't help this paranoia. And what hope have I got of calming down and getting things into perspective when the media run a constant campaign to top up my terror of everything – superbugs, terrorism, murderers, child molesters. You name it and I have to read about it or watch it on the telly. If it's not detective series about deranged killers, or crime series about post mortems, it's terrifying programmes about freak weather accidents. Nowhere feels safe. Everyone is frightened to go out. Muggings, it seems, are two a penny. It's all rather desperate, and I have a nasty feeling that the older I get, the worse it is going to become.

Occasionally, *Crimewatch* feels guilty about turning us all into nervous wrecks and does a retrospective of all the crimes it helped solve in the last series, making suggestions about how we can avoid similar crimes. This is not because they want to be helpful, but because they want to scare us all over again: scaring people gets good ratings. And *999* does hour-long updates of some of the juiciest disasters it has covered, with some practical advice as to what to do if your family is involved in a freak accident with a cement mixer and a swarm of killer bees. Or there's a quick reminder of what to do if you are dangling over a cliff with only a Safeways carrier bag to make into a parachute. They make it look like they are being constructive and helpful, but of course they are really just fuelling our fear, making us even more anxious about everything. I can't even turn the kitchen blender on without visualising someone getting their hand stuck in it. And I haven't been able to bring myself to use the waste disposal unit for years.

Anyway, accidents aren't like that. What's much more likely to happen is that one day you take your eye off the ball and slip on some turkey fat with the Sunday roast in your hand and do yourself a nasty injury on the kitchen floor. Everyone else would probably think that was really funny. And then, when they'd stopped laughing, they'd probably tell people you 'had a fall'. Because when you get to my age you don't just fall over – you have a fall, for some reason.

And all those self-help books don't help. You bring home *The Little Book of Calm* or *100 Ways to Lead a Calmer More Creative Life* or *How to Talk So That People Listen* or *Who Moved My Cheese?* and you enjoy the first chapter, think this is really going to do the trick. It's like a new religion for about half an hour, and then, of course, it all falls apart because life does not conform to rules. The more you focus on trying to get your life in order, the worse it gets. It's like the relaxation bit at the end of yoga and pilates classes: I get so self-conscious about my breathing and trying to relax that I can't relax at all. I get *more* stressed out.

WHERE'S THE FUN?

So you can see how tricky it is to have fun. What are we Grumpies to do? You can't go out clubbing all night (too tired), you can't get yourself an affair (too fat) – it's all so dull.

I indulge in silly little fantasy crushes. I've got a crush on the man who runs the aquafit session at the pool at the moment; ideal, since I am up to my neck in water and can go to the front like teacher's pet, whirling about in the water with my double chin stretched out so he can hardly see it. I have to make sure I get there before he sets up the ghetto blaster on the side – so that he doesn't see the heaving mass of my body, which is normally submerged. That way I can fantasise about us having urgent sex at his place. He is tall and lanky and gorgeous. And about 32 … Yes, right! Maddeningly, I got to the aquafit class a little too late last time I went, and he was already by the side of the water, so I had to dive in for the first time in 20 years to get my body under water as soon as possible. I made such a horrible noise with my belly flop that the lifeguard and gorgeous teacher insisted that I get out and fill in a silly accident report, despite my insisting that I was perfectly all right (I was so *not* all right). Now I can cross the hunky aquafit instructor off my fantasy list. Sometimes people can be so annoyingly helpful.

Not that it's any surprise that *anyone* is obsessed with sex, since sex is everywhere, all the time. At the moment you can't cross our road without seeing a huge poster of a pre-orgasmic woman advertising Trojan condoms. These days you can't turn on an episode of *The Bill* without seeing someone giving a blow job. It'll be on *The Antiques Roadshow* next. Is there no escape? It's all so vulgar, so in your face.

What happened to having crushes on one another, getting bashful and embarrassed on the first date, the slow build to the first kiss and beyond? Now I'm sounding like Barbara Cartland, but I wonder whether, when you jump into bed with one another on the first date, you miss out on all that. But now I'm sounding like Steve Wright on *Sunday Love Songs*, and I'd have preferred to stick with Barbara Cartland.

People now talk freely and frequently about blow jobs – a far cry from the scale we had at school. Kissing was number one, petting on top was number two, and on it went in graphic detail, ending with going all the way at number ten. A blow job, if it was talked of at all, was *after* number ten – really, really rude, really, really taboo. But now people walk about wearing T-shirts saying 'Fancy a Blow Job?' I recently saw a repulsive message on a young boy's shirt. It said: 'All I want is a blow job and a beer, what's wrong with that?' A lot is wrong with that, actually. And does he think that it will make people want to give him a blow job? Call me old-fashioned, but it has never really been my idea of a nice end to the evening. To be serious for a minute, it seems to me that it's men who gain from this, not women. I remember some ghastly article in *Cosmopolitan* saying that the calorific value of a blow job is about the same as a ham sandwich. I don't know a woman on earth who wouldn't prefer the ham sandwich. 'And they call it women's lib,' I can hear my mother saying. I think I know who gets the better deal from it.

Thank goodness I am not on the dating market. Can you imagine how awful that would be? It was bad enough dancing round your handbag at the disco with your girlfriends, hoping that someone might come up to you and ask you to dance, but imagine having to do the running yourself. I would never be able to read the signs right. I was always absolutely hopeless at that. Someone would spend months picking their moment while pretending they were interested in amateur dramatics and then pounce on me for a kiss, and I would be absolutely flabbergasted. On the other hand, I went to football circuit training for months on end every Wednesday evening because I had a crush on a certain person, and he never twigged. Let's face it, things would have been a lot easier for me if I could just have said – well, whatever you do say in those circumstances; perhaps, 'Would you like to come to the pictures with me next week, or something?' But then he might have said no, not next week, or the week after, or ever, so bog off, and then I would never have been able to pluck up the courage to ask anyone else out ever again. So on the whole I am relieved that unless I am suddenly catapulted back on to the dating market, I can cross all that off my to-worry list. That's one thing at least.

It would be the same if I had an affair: I wouldn't know the rules. I'd probably get all clingy and over-emotional, and anyway, where on earth would you find to do it? Presumably you both might have a bit of trouble doing it at your place, and doing it in a car has never been my idea of fun. Then you might have to go and hire a hotel room for the afternoon or something sordid like that. If you lived in Tokyo you wouldn't have to worry as they have love hotels made for the job, where you can both park your cars under cover in case your partner drives past and comes in to find you. But what on earth would you say to the woman on reception in this country if you wanted a room for, let's say, a couple of hours (or half an hour, let's be honest). Can I hire it for an afternoon meeting – nudge, nudge? Then they'd go and give you the conference room or somewhere else without a bed, and a large table laid out with neat little pads and pencils. They'd be forever coming in and checking whether you were all right for flip charts or Malvern water. It would all be too difficult.

And the telly is nothing *but* sex. It's not even as if you can just try to avoid the sexy dramas on after the watershed – the ones where they do that announcement at the beginning warning that the programme contains strong language and scenes of a sexual nature from the beginning (which is just their way of making sure you don't turn over). Sex is everywhere. It's in the ad breaks as well … especially in the ad breaks. Sex sells cars, shampoo, creosote (well, not creosote then). The message is, 'buy this car and you will have urgent hot sex on the beach within a minute of driving it out of the garage; you'll sneak out of work in your lunchtime for passionate shagging'. And then you buy one and nothing happens. And it's all so embarrassing when you're sitting there minding your own business with your aged mother and your teenage kids and some erection comes on the screen or people start kissing with tongues. I hate the way they kiss on screen these days. I liked it better in *Brief Encounter* – lips closed tight and lots of work with the shoulders. These days actors kiss and you can actually see their tongues going into each other's open mouths. Who needs it, I say.

HELL IS OTHER PEOPLE

You get invited to the odd party, but parties are utterly pointless if you're not on the pull. You spend the whole evening wanting a nice sit down or a proper meal instead of some canapés that you have to balance on the edge of your (very small) plate. And everyone is so polite and full of dreary small talk about their children, their new extension or their garden designers.

It's not even as if you can get drunk any more. Two glasses of wine and you're legless. More than that and you are heading for the hangover from hell. I can always tell when I am heading for a hangover: I fold my clothes up and put everything away, cleanse and tone my face before getting into bed and generally try to convince myself that I am not drunk at all … which is a sure sign that I am going to end up in casualty the next day.

And sicking up on the school run is not a good thing. The worst thing is when you prime yourself to have a night out on the town, really go for it, and it's all over by 10.30 and you are ready for bed.

Dinner parties are supposed to be what we do for fun. I've got to be honest and say that I really can't be bothered. I'd rather be at home, watching the telly or reading a good book. You only get stuck talking to some dreary banker, or the woman who runs the local council and bores for England.

On the rare occasion that I'm at a dinner party, or a do of some sort, my children die of embarrassment. I will actually say, 'Look, I'm very old and I'm very bored with you all, and I'm leaving.' It's one of the advantages of ageing – you can be eccentric and rude.
Sheila Hancock

It's not just that people bore you more easily, but you also get more restless; it's hard to sit still and know you won't get anything crossed off the to-do list for hours on end. And the trouble is, when you are at a dinner party you can't go home when you want to. It's not like going to the theatre or the cinema when you can (and I frequently do) walk out at half-time if it's not entirely stunning. I know when I'm bored in the theatre because I start to make a mental picture of the contents of my fridge, or run though all the things I have to do tomorrow. What I hate is when you go to the theatre and there's a sign that says there are two intervals. This play is going to be so-o-o long, so very, very long that they have to give you two intervals – it's enough to make you run away. Once you have – literally – lost the plot, you are stuffed. Unless it's opera or ballet, when there isn't any plot to speak of in the first place. You sit there fighting back the yawns and feeling wretchedly uncomfortable, thinking that this is a part of your life that you are never going to get back. You're longing to be sitting on your own settee watching the telly. So you leave at the interval, letting the other poor suckers stay for the second half, while you go and get a table at the restaurant or return home to your jim-jams and a nice cup of cocoa.

Of course, if you are at someone's house at a dinner party and they have evidently slaved over the coq au vin, you are well and truly stuck. The man next to you has told you all about his job in such minute detail that you even know about the Winnie-the-Pooh socks he wears on dress-down Friday. He hasn't asked you one single thing about yourself, assuming that either you are a stay-at-home mum and therefore able to answer only something stupefyingly dull, such as, 'Who's looking after the little ones tonight, then?' or that anything you say would be infinitely less interesting than hearing about the contents of his anorak pocket. You might be bored rigid – well, you *will* be bored rigid – but you still have to wait at least until the coffee before you can politely leave. Then some idiot launches into the longest story in history just as the hostess is about to make the coffee – you were on the home straight – and you get stuck for another half hour. When you do actually leave you have to pretend you want to see them all again – God forbid they take you seriously.

I can't even say any more that we have the babysitter to rush back for. This was always code for 'I am bored'. If it gets really, really bad you can always pretend your back's bad or your lumbago is playing up. See, you couldn't do that if you were in your 20s; that's one advantage of being older. When you get really old you can be brutally open and say you're bored, wave your walking stick at people and scare the hell out of them.

I don't even like people visiting me much. And I certainly wouldn't be stupid enough to *give* a dinner party. But sometimes visitors arrive *without* being asked. I can honestly say that I have never opened the door to unexpected visitors and been genuinely pleased. I can't think of any visit by any single guest that would not have benefited from a spot of prior notice. Everyone else seems to think it is so much fun. There they stand on the doorstep with some flowers and an excited grin on their faces saying, 'Surprise! We were on the M6 and Cheryl suddenly realised we were within 10 miles of your house, so here we are! I hope we're not interrupting anything … ' 'Oh, no, not at all … ' I lie, and in they all troop. Because the other problem with uninvited guests is that they travel in packs and never ever go. You allow great huge pauses to occur in the conversation, half-heartedly offer more coffee, which they accept when they know full well you want them to bog off home.

Now I'm well into my 40s and time is tangibly running out, I'd sooner slob around at home in my tracksuit bottoms than make polite conversation with people I don't like all that much. Every time someone drops in I promise myself that next time I'm going to do what Beryl Reid used to do when someone she didn't like rang the doorbell on the off-chance of finding her in. She'd leave it a few minutes, put her dressing gown on and say apologetically that she was in bed with someone she didn't know very well. Bull's-eye! Some people apparently ran down the path and wouldn't come back without giving several months' notice.

Either that or I could have a sign on the gate saying, 'No Surprise Visitors', like stuck-up people who have ones that say, 'No Casual Callers'.

The thing that I really do find fun now is staying in. In fact, I have turned it into an art form. I soak in the bath, then put on my dressing gown and some cosy woollen socks, draw the curtains, get myself a packet of crisps and a glass of wine and loll about on the sofa. I read the paper, get all stuck up

about bad TV and generally enjoy my own company. Nice. No, *really* nice.

Being home on a Friday night with the old man, an Indian take-away and a nice bottle of wine, and there's something on the telly, oh, I like that. I'm in my dressing gown, I mean it's not a weird dressing gown, it's not one of those quilted old lady ones. It's Cath Kidston. It's quite a funky dressing gown … don't get me wrong, I'M NOT THAT OLD.

Jenny Eclair

CHAPTER SIX

Get me the manager

THE ONE THING that makes all women of a certain age properly angry is shopping and service (or lack of it) in shops. Shopping has become a lot more annoying than it used to be. Grumpy Old Women are unable to be patient for one second. The moment I arrive at a shop counter or till I demand something happens immediately. I never look for anything myself on the shelves, but skid up to the nearest assistant and demand informed attention. And if I don't get it, I scream and scream until I am sick.

I have far too much to do, and far too little time to do it, so standing in queues gets me full-on, top-of-the-range grumpy. Apart from anything else, everyone keeps bringing out these books called *1000 Things to Do Before You Die* or *3000 Places to See Before You Die*, adding to the pressure and stress to cram as much in as I can before the inevitable, and increasingly closer, day when I fall off my perch.

First of all, I want to be treated with respect. On a bad day I want to be called Mrs or, dare I say it, madam, certainly not pet, or sweetheart, or love.

'Do you mind not calling me "love"? Would it really put you out at all if you called me Professor Greer? Would that really hurt?' But then

they think, 'Uh-oh, she's a crabby old thing. Now we'll treat her with kid gloves …'

Germaine Greer

The sort of service I want in shops is someone who can recite the entire manual to me, and explain quietly and sensibly how to use the thing I am about to buy and why I should buy it. I like to glide about the shelves with one (or ideally two) assistants fussing about at my hem, with them pulling goods out of drawers, making informed and clever suggestions as to why I should buy the one in the black rather than the one in the red, or solving whatever other dilemma is preoccupying me at the time. I like them hanging on my every word. I like them bringing me stuff that's still in its wrapper; I like them taking me to the pay point and pushing the other less important customers out of the way. I like their full-on attention until I leave the building, like I'm Audrey Hepburn or Madonna.

I get furious with people who don't serve me immediately, if I think they're not doing anything. If they're sort of closing drawers or checking lists or something, and they don't serve me immediately, I want to kill them. I just want to leap over and throttle them.

Dillie Keane

The rage that happens in shops happens, normally, because of bad service. There's appalling service in Britain. Appalling. I mean unimaginably dire service, and we all put up with it. Bored shop assistants who are either on the phone or talking to their friend, or, I've noticed recently, writing things down in a really illiterate hand.

India Knight

I say sarcastically cruel things to the assistants if they don't serve me the moment I appear on their radar. I say things like, 'Do you think if you took more interest in your job that you might enjoy it more?' or 'Is there any danger of you putting yourself out at all and doing what I think you are paid to do?' I generally sound and look like the customer they were all told about at customer training day. The one who behaves like Margaret Thatcher and needs careful handling. Sometimes in Ladies' Separates I feel like I'm inconveniencing them by being there at all. And some of them are old enough to know a great deal better. And the joy when they say to you that they haven't got it. 'No call for it', they say. Well, I'm bloody calling for it, you little madam.

I'm always in a hurry, obviously, so I like those automatic doors as it saves me .0003 of a second. If the assistant is busy chatting or doing anything else, or even with another customer, it niggles the hell out of me. I slap my bag on the counter to make a point. I can't bear it when the phone rings and they go off to deal with that first. Look, anyone can phone, but I am actually here, in the flesh, so in my view I get priority – right?

I think it should be acceptable to smack the shop assistants who don't serve us well, or are lippy or cheeky. But it can backfire …

The thing about being viciously vile to people is that it can backfire. I've had instances where I've just gone for somebody. The inner bully has leapt out and I've savaged somebody. And they've taken it, you know, me with my horrible screwed-up, spitty face, and then, at the end of it, they've said, 'I used to really like you; I was a big fan. I used to think you were really funny. I don't like you any more, and I'm going to tell all my friends what you're really like.' And then the shame hits you, and then, oh you're deflated. I spend most of my time puffing my ego up, puff, puff, puff, till I'm this big ego thing …

but it doesn't take much for it to be pricked, and then I'm just this deflated, shrivelled, shamed old woman with a bit of wee running down my legs.

Jenny Eclair

It's not just buying stuff that makes me annoyed. Taking it back is worse. When you get to the front of the Exchange and Refunds queue at M&S after a good 40 minutes of seething anger, they spend at least two or three minutes putting it all back on the hanger and re-labelling it while you're drumming your fingers on the counter. Once you have secured your refund (this is important, especially if you have a dark guilty secret, like you have in fact worn it for an entire summer and have just gone off it), you complain that they have wasted your time fiddling about re-marking the item for the shop floor when they could have released you into the outside world and done it later.

If I take something back, I wait to see whether the assistant uses the word 'sorry', as in, 'I'm sorry you had to trek all the way back here and queue for 40 minutes to return our shoddy goods that shouldn't have been shoddy in the first place …' If they don't use that magic word, I go into full-on apoplectic rage that the people at the back of the queue can hear. I turn into Margaret Rutherford or Margot from *The Good Life*. I am the battle-axe from hell, and I don't care who sees me. I let rip and demand to see the manager, which just makes the assistant in question dawdle even more.

Some of us are so worked up in shops that even when they *do* give you a refund without dawdling or fiddling about and annoying you, that's not good enough either …

The really annoying thing about it is when you're ready for a fight and you've worked out your argument, and you've got your shoddy bit of goods that you're taking back, then somebody's incredibly nice and really helpful, and they give you a full refund in about 23 seconds. That really annoys me too.

Kathryn Flett

I adore it when they offer you a store card at the end of the transaction, as they are told to, and you can say 'no' in an emphatic, vaguely disgusted sort of way. Or you say you don't *want* the receipt or no, you don't *want* a bag. Anything to be awkward. Anything to vent my anger.

When they ask me to fill in my name and address on some stupid form they have I always put someone else's name. If I am in a particularly bad mood, I put down the name of the woman two doors away from me, who is so houseproud that she has one of those stupid covers with autumn leaves on her wheelie bin – I mean, really, how sad is that? Still, now she'll have a few more catalogues coming through the door to fill up her wheelie bin.

SUPERMARKET HELL

Shopping for shoes you can choose to do or not, but shopping for food you have to do, and the one shop that gets us all down the most is the supermarket. I seem to spend most of my time in the wretched place. The first thing that annoys you is that the car park is the size of an Olympic stadium, and a good third of it is taken up with bays for disabled people and those shopping with small children. The rest of us have to catch a shuttle bus to get to the front door. They make you fiddle around with pound coins to liberate the trolley, which I have to admit I always find a bit challenging. It's not that I am stupid, it's just that I can never really figure out how to do it, so I have to hang around for someone to return theirs so that I can just give them the pound coin.

So in you go with your list, or more often than not without it because you have left it in the kitchen. You get to the fruit, flowers and veg first. Great idea! So when you get to the tins of baked beans and boxes of washing powder you have to either lift all your fruit and veg out, or put the heavy stuff on top so that the soft stuff gets squashed. The kettles, duvets and all the stuff that no one in their right mind wants are near to the checkouts, presumably because you will be tempted (as if), and they're ideally placed to stack on top of the eggs.

Have you noticed that supermarkets package everything to suit them, not you? You want red peppers, but they only sell them in threes – one red, one yellow and one green. You can't get just red peppers. The vegetables on offer are an appalling example of economic development gone bonkers: mini carrots, sweetcorn and asparagus in neatly wrapped packs from Zambia. Picked before they are fully grown. Stupid sugarsnap peas that have been airlifted across the world in cargo planes that have belched out enough carbon dioxide to fill a hangar, sent on a huge lorry and up the M6, belching out more carbon dioxide en route.

The things that make the blood come into my eyes are things like being offered tiny vegetables that have been grown in Zambia or Kenya or Zimbabwe that I know are being toiled over by women who have lost their own land. I don't want baby sweetcorn, I don't want 6-inch-long beans, tiny little things, with the red dirt of their homeland on them. I just feel really polluted and manipulated by the supermarket into wanting things that are so intolerable. Crops that should not exist.

Germaine Greer

And stop giving us all this packaging on everything. Every item of organic produce has about three layers of packaging, some ghastly eco-unfriendly polystyrene tray, some clingfilm that needs piercing with a sharp knife and then some posh cardboard nonsense on the outside. Stop it!

I hate the fact that they're supposed to be open 24 hours. What that means is if you go at ten at night, there's only one checkout open, so it takes you just as long as if you went at four o'clock in the afternoon.
Germaine Greer

And why is it so cold in supermarkets? Everything is in chillers, except the cat litter and the odd washing-up brush, so the whole place is absolutely perishing. You need your fleece on to go into the freezer section. If you go in a summer dress and some sandals, you'd best take one of those aluminium survival blankets with you in case you get held up at the till.

What's more, supermarkets are making an obscene amount of money out of us. They have their bonus card system, which is their sneaky way of getting your name and address to add to their wretched mailing list. You save all their coupons that come through the post and clog up your purse, and then, when you do remember to present them at the till, they are either out of date, or save you 5p on a box of firelighters, in July. And then they offer you computer vouchers for schools, and you think, oh that's good, but then you read that the supermarket is making £60 billion profit a year and you'd be more impressed if they actually gave away computers not computer vouchers.

You know that all those 'buy one get one free' special offers are designed to flog stuff they don't want any more, or to trick you into doing something you didn't want to? Like at the coffee place at the station, where the other day they had a coffee and bacon sandwich deal for £1.50. Coffee on its own costs £1.60. 'Can I have the coffee but no bacon sandwich for £1.50, please?' 'I can't sell you it without the bacon sandwich.' 'Yes but I don't want the bacon sandwich. I've already eaten breakfast.' 'I can't put it through the till otherwise.' So you have to have the bacon sandwich too – and then we're told we're the fattest nation in Europe.

MAKE YOUR MIND UP

And all this shopping takes so long, and one of the reasons it takes so long is that there is so much choice. Everything you buy or do involves far too much choice. Vast amounts of supermarket space are now devoted to what was once just a box of Daz or Omo. Now all manner of products exist that you can put into your washing machine – biological, non-biological, organic, hypo-allergenic – or things with stupid nets and balls, liquid gels, sprays, rinsers, fresheners … the list is endless, and is infinitely more expensive, more time-consuming and less environmentally friendly than buying a box of Daz and being done with it. Huge amounts of products clog up your pantry and your brain, and annoy the hell out of you. You can't just pop into the sandwich shop for a ham sandwich. It's avocado and Brie with rocket salad, and the queue is endless because everyone has to be asked 'white or brown, granary or wheat, rocket or lettuce, mayo or butter … ' Then you get to the drinks counter, and it's cappuccino or machiato, large, small or medium, soya or skimmed, chocolate or cinnamon on the top. It all takes about three times as long as it should do, and you come out wondering whether you made the right choice. Because the thing about choice is that it's unsettling. You might have been better with the avocado and grape, or might have preferred the soya milk … It all becomes such a big deal, whereas if you just went in and there were ham or cheese and pickle sandwiches, and plain tea or coffee, you'd have so much more room for other things in your brain.

The burden of too much choice doesn't even end when you get all your shopping home. Your washing machine has enough programmes to warrant a manual that is only intelligible to members of Mensa, so you only ever use one wash cycle which is the least likely to tie-dye the entire wash. But that doesn't mean it *doesn't* tie-dye everything anyway …

Even housework is subject to a massive amount of product choice, which means that you are now loaded down with sprays, mousses, polishes, all kinds of dusters, wet wipes and dry wipes … It's all so bulky that you need a golf buggy to cart it around the house. What's wrong with a duster? It's the same with everything – cars, hairdryers, beauty products. There is so much choice that you don't know where to start. It takes you ages to choose something, then you get it home

and immediately think you have made the wrong choice. It's not even as if the shampoo for brittle, hard-to-manage hair is any different from the one for fly-away and frizzy hair. They still just wash it. No more, no less.

You buy a car and you have to read the *Which?* report first, then some feature articles you saved from the *Mail on Sunday*, then you waste three Saturdays in a row talking to hideous people in car showrooms, and then you drive one home and wonder whether you should have gone for a hatchback after all.

Just stop giving us so many choices and decisions over things that really don't matter. In the old communist states you had just one sort of flat, one sort of car and one sort of bedspread. Think of the time and energy that limited choice would free up in one fell swoop. Buy things when they wear out rather than when you think they are a bit passé, or a bit not-you any more; buy a new car when the old one conks out. Marvellous.

Financial services are easily the worst culprits in the sea of choice. You go to the building society to make a simple transaction and they say, 'You know, you could be getting a lot more interest with a different savings account. This one is absolutely useless.' (They didn't say that when you opened it.) And they persuade you to make an appointment to come in so that they can tell you about all the wonderful options available. Making the appointment takes ten minutes because they have to print out a stupid letter and ask you loads of questions, and you get more and more fed up, then they send you another letter of confirmation in the post (how much did that cost?). So you go in and it takes an hour and a half to discover that the increased interest is likely to amount to about 45p in any one financial year. *Stop giving me all these choices. I am not interested.* I would prefer it if you could just arrange things so that I could actually phone the bank when I need to, not go through their ridiculous time-consuming central clearing system, which is simply their way of cutting costs.

RESTAURANT NIGHTMARES

The other place that bad service is hideously apparent is in restaurants. Either it takes an hour and a half to serve you half a melon, or there are waiters at your elbow fussing and fannying about every five minutes. It can still take an hour to get the half melon, but it costs ten times as much. There doesn't seem to be a happy medium.

The kind of service I find absolutely frustrating is the sort when they hover around you and there's always a waiter right here. You might be

having a conversation with your best girlfriend about her hysterectomy,
marriage breakdown, affair with Justin Timberlake – it could be
anything at all. And there'll be some bloke hovering, saying, 'And are
you ready to eat, madam?' 'No, we're not. We're not ready to order.
We don't want to order drinks. Go away. She's just about to tell me
the meaning of life. It's a really key moment. How thick is your skin?'
That's bad service. Doesn't happen in Le Gavroche.

Kathryn Flett

My sort of restaurant is one of those Chinese buffets that cost
about £10 and you can just go and help yourself to as much
prawn toast and sweet and sour pork as you like, and you're
back at home with your feet up in no time at all with no washing
up to do. But then I'm exceedingly unsophisticated. I even pick
my nose a lot when I'm driving. Get the picture? Again, I don't
want too much choice. I don't want to have to read through
three pages of starters, four pages of main courses and a
separate menu for puddings. Plus a specials board. It all takes
too long, and then you just don't know what you fancy, and in
the end it all becomes too significant. Probably most of the
stuff on the menu would be nice to very nice. And anyway,
common sense tells you that if they have a choice of 15 main
courses, they haven't got 15 gifted chefs toiling away over
them all – they are straight from the freezer and put in the
microwave five minutes before they are on your plate. Get real.
Mind you, I can order something straightforward and some
idiot dining with us might go and order a soufflé (20 minutes'
preparation time, according to the menu), which is code for
'you'll be there all night'. That makes me annoyed.

My impatience in restaurants is getting worse. It infuriates
my family, as I can't rest until the order is taken into the
kitchen and given to the chef. I can't bear it when the waiter
takes your order, then goes to another table and takes theirs

before putting it through to the kitchen. I feel like snatching it out of his hands and pinning it up in front of the chef myself. All my impatience is entirely counter-productive, as it ensures that the waiter ignores every signal I send for attention. He probably tells the chef to make sure everyone else gets their starters before I do.

When I first started going out to restaurants the Berni Inn craze was at its height, and that was nice and straightforward. You had the plaice, or the duck à l'orange, or the steak. They all came with peas and either chips or baked potato. Black Forest gateau or apple pie to finish, and some coffee with an After Eight mint. Nice. Now the menus are so pretentious that they're incomprehensible.

PONCEY MENU NAMES	BUT ON YOUR PLATE
• Neige of parsnip	• Mashed parsnip with a knob of butter
• Cappuccino of peppers and rocket	• Mixed salad without tomatoes
• Quartet of tomatoes	• Mixed salad with tomatoes
• Pan-fried cheese soufflé with field fungi	• Cheese on toast with mushrooms
• Confit of farm-reared pork with organic apple melange	• Roast pork dinner just like they serve in the pub, but at twice the price
• Freshly squeezed orange juice	• Freshly opened carton of orange juice
• Slow-roast guinea fowl	• Old boiler chicken ponced up a bit with a rich red sauce.
• Rhubarb concentrate with bechamel sauce à la maison	• Looks like the dog's been ill on your plate

As I get older, I find complaining easier and easier, more and more enjoyable.

I have become more vocal in my complaining. I now say, 'This is not working for me.' This is my new sentence. You smile, because of course it's very easy to sound like a psycho when you are complaining. But if you smile and say, 'I'm sorry, this isn't working for me,' you usually get quite a positive reaction. If your dinner is disgusting and the waiter comes and says, 'Was that all right?' normally you say, 'Yes, thank you, it was lovely,' even though you had to gag and leave it all on the plate. But if you say, 'No, it didn't work for me,' it's of course horribly American, but it seems to be quite a good middle way. It's not too aggressive and it's not too passive. It's just letting them know that it's all about you, and for you it's not working.'

India Knight

And as for tipping. Let's just ban it.

Everything aimed at adults is organic this or fresh and seasonal the other, yet when it comes to children's menus, restaurants are prepared to serve up the kind of gunk that looks as appetising as pet food. Why do people consider it acceptable to feed children with chemically enhanced and genetically modified turkey droppings and chips washed down with dayglo drinks when the adults are offered perfectly nutritious menus? Revolting bits of reconstituted meat that have been lying on the factory floor, along with turkey bottom and genitals, are made into friendly kiddie shapes so that children eat them all up. Novelty cheese products full of E numbers and additives, and juice drinks that are little more than coloured sugar water are peddled with unscrupulous zeal. Then we wonder why our children are getting fat. Wonder why they like fast food and don't eat enough spinach or fresh fruit. It all makes me properly annoyed.

CHAPTER SEVEN

Getting out and about

TRAVELLING IS SO MUCH MORE UNPLEASANT than it used to be. Even taking a straightforward trip on the train is irritating beyond measure. If I need to get to London, and sometimes it is unavoidable, I have to set aside a morning to navigate my way through the telephone booking service (unless I want to pay full fare, which is literally the same price as a new winter coat), and I have to get there a good 20 minutes before the train leaves to make sure I get a space in the smallest, most expensive pay and display car park in the world, which is so greedy that the bays are the width of a single bed. When I get on the train it smells of sewage (apparently they don't have time to empty the waste tanks more than once a day … nice!), and there are so many cases in the aisles that everyone is hemmed in between Julian from foreign marketing and Sharon who is dumping her boyfriend, or having phone sex with him – or both at once. Julian has turned the tiny table you have to share between four of you into his dreary office, and is going through some spreadsheets with his team back at base, discussing sales targets and boring everyone to death with details of the forthcoming away day. Sometimes I think I might lean over and say, 'Sorry, I hadn't realised this was your office. I thought it was a train, silly me.' But they'd just write you off as a nutter and carry on. What's happened to a little reticence? Trouble is, after all this huffing and puffing someone from the office usually rings *my* mobile, and I have to answer and sort out their problem, which means I lose all credibility as the mobile police, and then have to make friends with Julian as everyone else in the carriage is scowling at me now.

Of course, the whole journey takes about an hour longer than you were anticipating. Last time I was badly delayed – something like two hours – the great British spirit came out. Everyone got talking, and I made a whole new set of friends; we're planning reunions and everything, so it's not all bad. Except I'd have preferred to have got there on time. Now I'll have to send these people Christmas cards.

The roads, too, are so much more irritating than they were. More cars, more traffic jams and more dithery motorists. Sometimes I just wish they sold those flashing blue lights at Halfords so you could put one on your car roof to push everyone out of your way, and get home faster to that glass of dry white and the double episode of *ER*. And what's with all the cyclists? Jumping the lights, hogging the centre of the road and generally being where you can't see them.

I suppose when I am driving, particularly in London, the thing that makes me angriest is cyclists, the anarchists of the road. Now, on the whole I like anarchists in every other sphere of life, I really like a bit of anarchy, but they go up on the pavement, they weave in and out, ignore traffic lights and then if you dare go anywhere near them, they scream at you like banshees. There's this extraordinary assumption that we all have to get out of their way. But they can do what they damn well like.
Sheila Hancock

They wear all that eco warrior gear, and Lycra shorts that squish their genitals up for all to see: it's so revolting. I think we should just be able to push them over when they get in our way – stick our hands out at the lights and push them right over. Get our own back.

But some of us use the car as an anger outlet, to just scream our heads off when no one is looking and no one can hear us.

When I'm in the car I can have a nice scream because I am contained. I scream very, very loudly, or I scream filthy words and nasty expletives, and nobody can hear. They think, 'What an odd woman!' but I am gone in a second, so it doesn't really matter.

Michele Hanson

Then you go on holiday to Cornwall and get into the longest traffic jam that anyone can remember. Not that holidays are quite what they used to be either. For my Grumpy Old Man, going on holiday means chucking a few T-shirts and shorts in a case, choosing a couple of novels at the airport and working late the night before we leave to clear his emails. For me, holidays start weeks before we go. I collect little piles of things, from mosquito spray to flip-flops, and start putting them all in the spare room months before the big day. Lists start to accumulate, as you'd expect, of tasks that have to be done *before I go*. They start off being totally unrealistic, such as 'Decide when to retire', or 'Redecorate the bathroom', and then they get less ambitious, but more urgent, such as 'Save enough money', and then they get totally and utterly last-minute must-do panics as in 'Book kennel for dog', 'Take dog to kennel', 'Make sure Leonie from down the road is booked to come in and feed hamster', 'Arrange to leave the milkman his money', 'Turn the immersion off', and so on … Then there are all the things you have to do to avoid being burgled, such as connecting lamps to those annoying time-switches to make the house look as if it is occupied when it isn't. They always take masses of fiddling with. And they are so stupidly obvious. If I was a burglar, I'd just look down the road to see who had left the landing light on and assume that they were either out for the evening or away on holiday. You might as well leave the keys out on the front mat.

All this, of course, is on top of the rush at work to get things done before going away, so I'm in a complete panic the week before I go. People learn to give me a very wide berth. Of course, because I do everything at top speed some little things do get overlooked. Like where I put my passport. A couple of years ago, the night before the big day, I looked in the drawer of my filing cabinet that says 'Important Documents', where I keep my passport. I have one of those filing cabinets with dozens of slim little drawers in it, where I put some of the vast array of personal admin that clogs up my life. One drawer says Medical, others say Bank, Insurance, Credit cards and so on. If you were an alien and landed in my study, you'd think I was astonishingly well organised, until you opened the drawers and realised that the only one with anything in it is labelled Miscellaneous and is full to bursting. So I looked in the Miscellaneous file, then in the Important documents file again just in case, and couldn't find my passport. Strange, I think. Oh well, it'll turn up. But no. Nothing, no passport.

I start to get all hot, ring the passport office, expecting to have to drive through the night to Cardiff to get a new one, only to be told that replacement passports take a week. What with terrorism and everything, a *full week*. I look at my mother's passport and wonder whether I could get away with it, and the answer is probably yes, but conclude that being in prison might be worse than being left behind. So left behind I was – the cruellest, most tangible example ever of me being in such a stupid rush all the time. I had to take the family to the airport and wave them all off to Antigua. Then I went home and moped for four days. I couldn't even say to myself, 'Oh well, I'll do some spring cleaning, then.' I just moped. I bought a packet of ten Silk Cut and moped until the replacement passport finally arrived and I could join them. Now my passport has its own drawer with a lock and key. If I knew where to buy one, I'd put it in an illuminated shrine on a red satin cushion – just like the revered relics of medieval saints and pilgrims that you see in churches abroad.

GET ME OUT OF HERE!

Trains are annoying enough, but planes are something else. The whole sorry business of flying is annoying. They get you out of bed at 4.30 a.m. and to the airport two hours early in order to maximise the window for shopping. Then, when you get to the front of the interminable queue at check-in, they waste everyone's time by asking you cunningly clever questions, such as, 'Are you carrying firearms?' or 'Did you pack your bag yourself?' That's really going to sort out the terrorists. And when you ask them to do something for you, such as giving you an aisle seat, they laugh, saying that all the aisle seats were booked in March, don't be silly!

The first problem for me and my Grumpy is that we are both used to being in charge at work, and we both have very different approaches to the whole business of flying. So the trouble starts immediately we leave home. I want to get to the airport in plenty of time, I want to get good seats, I need to allow plenty of time for all my tedious pre-flight routines, plus I have to go to the loo about four times before I board because I don't like it when there's turbulence, and I *really* don't like it when I'm in the loo and there's turbulence, so I have to get all that over with. I like to have plenty of room to put all my things in the overhead lockers and so on. And then I like to get one of the blankets and the headsets and get settled. The kids are the same as Grumpy, so they come racing to the gate as cool as you like at the last minute, and get exactly the same room in the overhead lockers and get one more blanket than me.

I get very edgy when I'm flying. I don't like taking off, I don't like the plane turning corners or wobbling about, and I don't like landing either.

And flying is the last unashamed example of the class system. Effectively, the gist of it is sit down and shut up for ten hours. The stewardesses might throw you some monosodium glutamate when they can get around to it, which will alleviate the boredom for about 12 minutes, if you're lucky. And when they have a minute between fanning the people in first, or doing manicures for the lady in business class with the frequent flyer card, they might be able to sell you some duty free. Chickens in transit have a more comfortable time. Then they insult you by suggesting you listen to the channel that has exercise suggestions for twirling your ankles and relaxing your neck muscles, which are not helpful or relaxing at all, but are all about minimising the risk of the airline being taken to court when someone gets DVT on a long-haul flight. Is it any wonder that people get DVT in economy class on a long-haul flight?

The whole class system is designed to make you feel inadequate if you are anything less than first class. If you do turn left at the top of the aircraft stairs, you are treated like gods. And I hate the way the stewardesses swish the curtains once you've taken off so that you can't even see what's happening in first class, as if to say, 'You lot at the back are riff-raff. These people are gods. If only you had worked that little bit harder, if only you had been that bit more successful, you'd be here, behind this curtain, too. But as it is, you are not even allowed a glimpse, so bog off and knuckle down to your nasty 12 hours of not even having enough room to bend down to get your bag off the floor. Oh, and if I get a minute, I might just be able to pour you a Diet Coke, but don't count on it.'

Perhaps the most insulting class is the one up from cattle class, which is called something stupid like economy plus or premium business. It means you have about a quarter of an inch more leg room than in economy, get some orange juice on take-off and a stupid blue label for your luggage. All this for just £800 extra per seat. They're having a laugh, aren't they?

It's like the *Titanic* all over again. I have a horrible feeling that in the unlikely event of the plane falling out of the sky, the first-classers would be given time to pack all their hand luggage neatly and finish their champagne and movie before the crew even got the escape chutes out for the rest of us. Mind you, we'd have our whistle and light for attracting attention, so that's good! First-class passengers probably have their own individual ejector seats. Everyone else would burn to a cinder.

It's no wonder people go to great lengths to be upgraded. They try everything – dressing up, dressing down, handing in medical certificates, plugging themselves into drips, feigning serious illness at the gate. They would even sell their own mothers. Sure, being upgraded on a long flight is no small matter, but the way they act you'd think it was a matter of life and death. It's all so hideous, and it brings out the worst in us. The whole one-upmanship thing is ugly. People endlessly tell you about near

misses, about their flight to Hong Kong, not because they are
being informative or interesting, but because they are desperate
to tell you how many air miles they have won, or how often
they have flown premium economy or some such nonsense.

Of course, someone who is as anxious as me finds flying
particularly challenging, especially when it looks so basic – like
the crudity of the windscreen wipers, which look as worryingly
flimsy as the ones on a Reliant Robin. What are they going to
do when one of them packs up in the middle of some storm
clouds over the Indian Ocean? Pull over?

The other day I was flying in to Stansted Airport and the
pilot came on to say that he wasn't qualified to land in fog, so
we had to go to Luton instead. What? Not qualified to land in
fog? It's like me saying on a motorway that I'm not qualified to
drive in rain. I wish he hadn't told us – for one thing, it looked
a bit foggy when we landed in Luton anyway.

I spend every flight on edge, which is a bit wearing when
it takes 18 hours. I look at the flight crew for signs of anything
out of the ordinary. I keep a keen lookout for anyone who is
likely to go mad with a bottle of whisky. I have been known to
go up to cabin crew and say, 'I can smell something strange,'
and get them all worried, only to be told it's the chicken tikka.
Or I report my suspicion that someone is smoking in the toilet,
then follow them in and have a good sniff round. It doesn't
help that on a recent TV programme – 'The Worst Flight of
My Life' or 'The Day I Nearly Died' or some such – they
showed you how people manage to smoke in the loo without
being detected: they use a pair of tights to cover up the alarm.

I worry about a fight breaking out over how much arm
room one person is giving another on the armrest; I worry about
things falling on top of me; I worry about turbulence breaking
the plane in half. Worry, worry, worry – I hate it. I have a little
washbag that contains my sad little flying kit – little things that

are comforting in a stupid sort of way: chewing gum for my
ears when landing, tissues in case I come up with some horrid
thoughts and have to touch wood, sleeping tablets to calm me
if we are plunging to our death … I can't fly without it.

It all amounts to a fear of pointless death. Dying on your
way to a stupid meeting about sales figures, or after a horrid
holiday with someone you've decided you don't like very much.

And the whole safety performance is pointless. They go
through their idiotic routine telling us – gosh, how amazing –
how to do up our seatbelt; like anyone is going to have trouble
with that! And even I can see that the plane is going to sink if
it falls out of the sky and lands on water; there will be no time
to get on that silly chute. Once you are airborne, the chute is
academic. The only time it might come in useful is if the plane
self-combusts while still on the tarmac. But even then I imagine
the fat bastard sitting in the exit row will just hold his very large
body in front of the door until he has packed up all his CDs,
and by then the rest of us will have turned into charcoal. So the
bit that I always dread is when they say you should look at the
card to see what position to adopt if you hear the word 'brace'.
Because I can imagine that. I can imagine trying to scribble
down notes to my nearest and dearest while plummeting out
of the sky and fighting the G-forces. They'd probably turn up
the hideous 'calming' musak, thinking that the up-tempo
version of 'Yesterday' would really help to calm you down.

And I wish they wouldn't keep coming on to the PA system
boring you with this, that and the other, all of which amount to
ways of encouraging you to use your Barclaycard. A PA system is
always a danger. People get a taste for it – like those who always
volunteer to run the auction at the PTA: you can never shut
them up once they get going. One very stuck-up British Airways
stewardess was particularly annoying recently. She had obviously
been demoted from long haul to taking the riff-raff to Tenerife

(we're talking applause on landing), so she would not leave the microphone alone. It was her way of making herself feel a bit more important than the other cabin crew. Every five minutes she was on about the charity box to throw your loose change in, or she'd update our flying time, go through British Airways' latest offers, car hire opportunities and perfume. She was so plummy that she sounded as if she'd got a tea towel in her mouth. In the end the pilot had to shut her up. I bet all the other stewardesses loathe her. She's probably on hovercrafts now.

FOREIGN PARTS

When we eventually arrive at our holiday destination, there's usually about an hour when everyone in the family is getting on, the sun is shining, and we are having a nice lunch, with nothing much planned for the afternoon. At that moment I am truly happy. But it's taken all this time for me to realise that as you grow older and more responsibilities and anxieties stick to the side of you, holidays do not live up to their carefree promise. Once you have children – even if they are teenagers – holidays are more work than staying at home, with the addition of calamine lotion, a tummy bug and a trip to the local police station or casualty department.

For a start, there are hundreds of new things to worry about. Invariably the hotel pool is on the side of a cliff, with no railings to prevent your toddlers from hurtling to their death. The pool doesn't have a shallow end, and the sea has jellyfish. The glass coffee table in the room has lethal corners and the kids keep slipping on the marble floor. Meanwhile, the childless couples at the hotel laze on the sun-loungers and read novel after novel, tut-tutting at any noise your children make. Then they stroll indoors at lunchtime, presumably for some afternoon nookie, while you're blowing up water-wings or looking for crabs in rockpools.

You wonder why you didn't just stay at home, where at least the kids have their video games and some telly to watch.

The Germans and the Swiss are up at 6.00 a.m. bagging the loungers in the shade or within a bus ride of the pool. Some of them bag one for the morning and another for the afternoon, according to where the sun is, so you have no choice but to join the race unless you want to spend the week next to the kitchen dustbins. Alternatively, you could be fully confrontational rather than just seethingly mad, and throw off their silly little towels and novels when they are at lunch and start an international incident. Each year I say to myself that I will rise above this pathetic system and not bag a sun-lounger all week. But in the end you get up at 7.00 and claim the last couple of loungers. But we didn't start the sun-lounger bagging system. They did.

All the other Europeans have better rooms than us: theirs overlook the pool or the sea but we are looking at the car park or are under the glass-crushing machine by the bar. It seems like whichever way you cut the cake, the British are pretty much at the bottom of the food chain. Even the rep looks like she's been round the block a few times. All this is very bad for overachievers like me. Once I have spotted which sun-lounger position is the best, it becomes a personal challenge to get it out of the hands of the enemy and put up a British flag by placing an Agatha Christie novel on it, or draping it with my sarong. You might catch the enemy unawares once, perhaps the morning after their tennis championship piss-up, but you can be sure the Germans won't let a gap like that develop in their lines again. It's the same story with the coach. Guess who gets the two best seats with all the leg room at the front? And guess who gets to the check-in queue at the airport first? The other Europeans have sussed it all out, you can be sure.

It's quite hard to be off duty on holiday. Everyone else is lolling about looking relaxed, and you're worrying about how well they rinse the salads, how long the chicken has been sitting in the sun, and how uneven the paving stones round the pool are.

I come into my own at the breakfast buffet, though. It'd take more than a few pushy Germans to put a stop to my game. I know you're not supposed to, and in some hotels they even have little signs trying to prevent you doing it, but the truth is that more ham and rolls leave the breakfast buffet in beach bags, ready to be eaten at lunchtime, than are eaten in the restaurant itself. Everyone knows what you're doing. You've already guzzled enough bacon and eggs for ten and then you start making ham sandwiches, as if you are going to find room to poke those down as well. Everyone else in my family complains about it bitterly and disowns me when I wrap them up in little napkins and sneak them into the beach bag, except they are all happy to eat them when I pass them a roll at the poolside later on. Sometimes I leave the restaurant quite blatantly carrying a banana to put the waiters off the scent. I'm not as bad as the Swedes, I've seen them coming out with a week's worth of cheese and ham sandwiches: they're probably selling them on the beach – opened their own outlet.

Of course, the more expensive the hotel and the more ripped off you feel, the more inclined you are to strip the place of freebies. I work hard at topping up my stockpile of shampoo and soap every day by ringing reception to say I have run out and asking them to send up some more. It's pathetic. Everything that is not nailed down goes into the case. I walk past the chambermaid's trolley in the morning and if she's not around, I nick some mineral water and more shampoo. It's not even very nice shampoo; obviously they have done that on purpose so that the Dutch and the Germans leave it alone, but not me.

I've stopped nicking the disposable slippers, though – they really are the most pointless items. You can't walk two yards in them without tripping up and they curl up in your suitcase

anyway. And I don't nick the tea bags or milk cartons either. OK, so I nick the tea bags, but not the milk. Well, only occasionally.

I know for a fact that I am not the only person to do this sort of thing because hotels have got wise to people like me. They now put notices in the bathroom saying, 'If you would like to purchase the dressing gown, £50 will be added to your bill', which is code for 'Don't even think of putting this in your case: remember we swiped your Barclaycard when you checked in.'

I'm mentally deducting what I've nicked off the cost of the holiday. It makes me feel slightly less ripped off. Slightly less angry about all the other nations getting the best rooms.

Everyone knows not to use the minibar because the tonic waters cost £7.50 each, and the Toblerone exceeds the cost of the holiday itself. So we Brits like to buck the system, and we spend each morning trekking to the local store on buses carrying back bottles of tonic water and Coke and working up a terrible sweat to get it back to our rooms when no one is looking. It costs exactly the same as the minibar, but we feel oh so smug.

I love the signs they give you to put on the door, such as 'Privacy please', which is obviously code for 'We're shagging', or 'Please make up my room', which is code for 'We've stopped shagging, so get your arse in here and make the bed'. I like to keep the 'Privacy please' one on the door to show off and make it look like Grumpy and I are at it all the time.

I am hugely antisocial on holiday. I spend my whole life having to talk to people on the phone, so I do not, emphatically do not, want to make friends. But other people – probably more normal people than me – do go on holiday and want to be sociable. There are couples who chum up with people and stay in touch when they get home! Couples who write their *real* address down when you do the exchange of contacts on the last day! You have to go to the ends of the earth to avoid these sorts of people. You have to scale mountains and take huge detours to avoid them at their favourite bar lest they come and ask, 'Do you mind if we join you?' Unfortunately, they have often sat down before you have a chance to say, 'Yes, we do mind, in fact.'

Then there's the weather to worry about and feel disappointed with. You can cope with rain and drizzle if you're in Weston-super-Mare because you will have packed your Pacamac and some join-the-dots puzzles, but in Tunisia it is a bit grim if the weather doesn't live up to the temperature chart in the brochure, and all the rooms are freezing and you've only packed shorts. Which ride up your bum, in my case. In the Lakes everyone trudges around in their wet anoraks not knowing what to do with themselves, or they go and look at the moped and motorcycle museum, or take a trip to Lakeland and buy some Tupperware … with all the other poor drenched sods who also wish they were at home in front of the telly.

CHAPTER EIGHT

Christmas

YOU THOUGHT YOU WERE GRUMPY most of the month, not even just at *that* time of the month, but Christmas comes around, or starts to come around in about September, and you realise that once again you are going to enter a very dark, very bleak tunnel of grump that lasts until 6 January, when the whole nightmare is over and you get the house back to normal.

As much as you think you like Christmas, and there are little bits of magic that in retrospect, and only in retrospect, almost make it worthwhile, the truth is that Christmas is just one long, long, long, long, long list of errands. One long, long, long list of shopping and carrying and fetching and cooking that all culminates in one action-packed and labour-intensive 24 hours – Christmas Day. All that work and energy has effectively been spent on one normal-length type day. And then on Boxing Day all the magic (such as there was) is gone, and Grumpy goes to the football match and your mother wants to go to the sales.

But do we learn? Do we ever just hang loose about Christmas and hey, let it all be chaotic and just unfold? Do we hell. Which is why at Christmas our grump reaches its climax.

In late August, just before the kids go back to school, when you're buying protractors and shin-pads and ink cartridges, you notice something in W.H.Smith's that you think must be a mistake. 'Christmas cards?' you guffaw. 'Who on earth is thinking about Christmas?' you exclaim to the assistants. 'We've sold about 50 today,' they say. You go home and start to ponder on just how little time there really is left till Christmas, and how very much there will be to do. So you make your first Christmas list, or deposit your first little pile of Christmas things in the spare room because once you think other women are starting to prepare for Christmas, sheer panic sets in. If they've started, then you have to start. Because the other thing about Christmas is that it all has to be perfect. The house has to look like something from *House and Garden*, the table has to look like Doris Day would have wanted it, and your food – obviously – has to look and taste like Delia's. So once you have set those sorts of standards, you can see how the panic takes hold.

Two weeks later you pick up *Good Housekeeping* in the doctor's waiting room and there is a four-page spread on 'The Countdown to Christmas'. There it all is, week by week going down to zero and 'the big day'. Hour by hour, minute by minute it describes exactly which tasks should be done when, be it pickling onions, making the Christmas pud, piping the meringues or putting up the holly. There it is – your life sentence for the next three and a half months. The standard by which you will judge yourself and your ability to be a domestic goddess, or simply a good woman. No one who has anything to do *other* than preparing for Christmas could possibly achieve the contents of this article. Christmas is a full-time job. And now you are going to have to fit it in along with everything else – the cleaning, cooking, ironing, shopping, seeing to the kids and ferrying everyone about. Oh yes, and work.

PRESENTS

You can't buy 20, 30, 40 presents and not make a list, so you have to do lists. It gets quite desperate – you've got to cook, you've got to decorate the house, you've got to buy the presents, you've got to wrap the presents … Lists upon list upon lists. Ticking, crossing off, making new lists – because I do need something to cross off. It's desperate …
Lesley Joseph

Your first list of presents fits on two pages of A4, but experience tells you that this list will get bigger and bigger as the weeks go on. More and more people will either send you a gift that you have to reciprocate, or one of the kids will come home and say that everyone else is giving the ballet teacher a present this year, so that's someone else to buy a box of chocolates for. Presents for your mother, your mother's mother, presents for your husband to give to your mother, his mother, presents for your mother to give to the kids, presents for you to give to the kids, and then all the presents for Santa to give to the kids. Plus presents for yourself that your mother has given you money to buy as she doesn't know what to get you.

You go to the stash of uninteresting and unsuitable rubbish that people have given you during the year and wonder what you can wrap up and get ticked off straight away. The washbag set from Marks and Sparks that you haven't opened, a disposable camera that came free with the dishwasher, that kind of thing. Once you've wrapped it up, you fret over who bought you the washbag set in the first place and hope it isn't the person you are about to give it back to, but the chances are that someone gave it to them anyway and they won't remember. You wrap these up and put them in the airing cupboard for safe-keeping. Then you get to 20 December and find them, having been looking for them for about a month.

Some people, like Maureen Lipman's mother, would recycle presents immediately after opening them.

My mother, God rest her soul, as soon as you gave her something, she would be eyeing it up to see who she could give it to when they turned up and she didn't have a present from them. You could see the virtual wrapping paper going around the thing you bought ... you could see it was on its way to Doris next door.

Maureen Lipman

Come November you can't turn on the radio for Christmas songs; Slade and Cliff Richard blare out all day just to remind you that time is running out. Every morning Terry Wogan tells you how many shopping days there are still to go before the big day.

The earlier I start on the serious shopping for presents, the worse the shops seem to be. By November the car parks are full, and the shops are heaving with women like me, clutching their lists, a pen and a stack of stuff from the Body Shop, dozens of pairs of slippers, and a dance mat or three. We're lugging it all back to the car and cramming it into the boot, then feeding the meter again to return to the fray.

To make matters worse, Delia or Nigella are full-on organised like a couple of bossy prefects, and tell you in October that it's high time you pre-froze the mince pies, or tie-dyed your cutlery in time for the big countdown.

By late October all the magazines and the *Daily Mail* are full of stunningly well-organised women pictured with their satin-dressed and perfectly coiffed children, looking like a picture-postcard Christmas. Everyone is getting ready. Getting slimmer, getting more perfect as we get nearer to the big day. Because the other thing that is so maddening for women at Christmas is that it all has to be so blooming perfect. It's no good just getting up on Christmas morning and lazing around in your dressing gown, having a perfectly relaxed and untidy day. Everything has to be perfect to be in any way successful. You can't just buy a bag of satsumas and be done with it: they have to have their leaves on, as they do in *House and Garden*, and be arranged aesthetically on the sideboard. Your presents have to be colour coordinated, and the napkins have to be tied up with mistletoe or some black ribbon with sequins … If only we could all just go to Iceland on Christmas Eve and bung a frozen turkey and some Black Forest gateau in the car, we'd all be much better company. But if you did, of course, you would consider yourself a failure.

Although I don't want Christmas to be until December, I do spend three months preparing for it, and I spend three months debriefing after it, so there's actually only six months of the year when I'm not doing Christmas. That's terrible.

Lesley Joseph

No one else seems to be taking the preparation at all seriously. Your Grumpy Old Man seems to sidestep all this precision planning without you really noticing. You hand him the neatly written list of presents that he needs to get and cards that he needs to write, but he doesn't seem to take it very seriously. The shops start to run out of Ken and Barbie Underwater Diving Sets that your youngest has written to Father Christmas for. And your Grumpy Old Man hasn't even started the shopping. For some reason, he is able just to get on with real life, get on with his job all through December and lead a normal existence until about lunchtime on Christmas Eve, when he scampers round John Lewis and throws some things into the boot of the car in a carefree fashion. *We*, on the other hand, spend most of December in a state of sleep deprivation, and ricochet between tears and throwing things at anyone who gets too near.

Men have got no reason to be grumpy at all, because they don't have to do anything. They really don't have to do anything. In fact, my husband goes out on Christmas Eve to buy my present. He's had 364 days to go and get it, and he goes on Christmas Eve to buy my present. They maybe do one trip to Argos and get one thing. My husband, like most men, can only do one thing at a time. If there's two cups of tea to be made, they'll make one. And then they'll make another one after that. If my husband's going to the shop and I say, 'Can you get a loaf of bread and a pint of milk?', he'll come back with one or the other. Never both.

Linda Robson

One year I handed my Grumpy a list of absolutely everything he needed to do for Christmas. It wasn't a lot, and it was very specific – things like 'buy coal for fire, firelighters, blue sweater for Uncle Dennis from M&S size 24', etc. I breathed a sigh of relief: I had handed some things over. I asked him how he was getting on with the list in mid-December and he said, rather lightheartedly, 'List? Oh yes, I haven't seen the list for ages. Have you got it or have I?' In other words he had lost the list …

But some people are cleverer than others with their list:

Because I am officer-in-command of the list I get to keep the fun jobs. So I get to make the cranberry sauce and my husband gets to put the Christmas tree up, find all the decorations, anything that involved fiddly things like replacing the light bulbs on the fairy lights. They get to do all that naff stuff and I get to do the fun stuff.

Jenni Trent Hughes

DECORATIONS

Then the house has to be got ready. Delia and fellow goddesses have already dried out flowers and sheaves of wheat and stuff, sprayed lavish room decorations, and created centre-points for the table and huge holly-laden things for the hall.

Obviously I make all my own Christmas garlands. And I've always got one going up the staircase and sort of wrapped round the banister – lovely dried fruit and sprayed apples. Spray all round the house. Yeah, right.

Arabella Weir

One year I got some of this gold and copper spray, and had to be physically restrained from spraying everything in sight. I sprayed the foliage and cones just as they'd done in the photo in *Good Housekeeping*, but then I wondered about the pot itself, the candles and the candleholder. Before you know it you've sprayed the entire dining room and hall, and it looks, well, a bit sparkly and ridiculous and tasteless. Then you have to get holly, but not just any holly. Oh no, it has to have berries on. So you grab your secateurs and stop your car on the side of busy dual carriageways and come back home with bags and bags of it that then have to be placed festively and tastefully all round the fireplaces and hall. That's November gone.

In December the kids are bleating on about a tree, so you can put off the trip to the loft no longer. You teeter on the stepladder into the loft and get down all the stuff you hurriedly shoved into boxes and bags last January, when everyone was bored to tears with the whole caboodle. It all comes down into the hall and looks tatty and broken, so you need to add some new lights to your list because the old ones have strangely entwined themselves like bindweed. You can't bring yourself to chuck out the nativity scene with cotton balls that your children made in reception; if you do chuck something out that they made at school last year, they only go and notice and you feel a right heel. The tree lights need an electrician because they keep fusing the house and Grumpy isn't around to fix them. You wish you weren't short-tempered because in the movies you do this bit by candlelight and be jolly festive about it.

Real Christmas trees really are a pain. You're still finding needles in July. The other thing is, we let the kids decorate the tree, and then, when they've gone to bed, we take it all off and do it again properly. We won't tell them though. I mean, they basically just throw things at the tree and see where they land.

Linda Robson

Still, the men can be trusted to take care of the tree – that's one thing they can be relied upon to do really well.

My husband always buys a tree that is too big for the room. Every single year without fail. So we have this routine where he brings the tree in and I take the children out – I have to remove them from the building altogether because his language is so appalling. He gets the tree in and it won't fit in the room because it's too big. He takes it back outside into the street, much to the bemusement of the neighbours. He starts hitting and kicking it Basil Fawlty-style, giving it a damn good talking to, before he saws about three feet off the top of it. Of course, that means there's nowhere to put the Christmas fairy. We never have a fairy.

Jane Moore

Sometimes men can be such girls.

GOOD CAUSES

And what is the point of it all? How have we become so removed from the spiritual message of Christmas?

I think the worst thing about Christmas is that it's become such a mess. I mean, we're supposed to be celebrating a simple humble birth in a poor stable, and we've got overtaken by greed and the panic of how much we are going to eat and how much we're going to drink, and it's just become about excess. And I think that's sad.

Sheila Hancock

The charity at Christmas ends up being another pressure, something else to worry about, and there's so much of it. In December the charity nightmare begins. Fund-raising reaches an all-time high, with Christmas fayres, tombolas and shoe boxes to organise. You foolishly offer to organise the PTA Christmas do at the local Italian, and spend 30 hours organising an event that raises about £10. It would have been cheaper and more efficient for everyone just to sign cheques and post them off. The school hall has a box the size of a washing machine for people to donate items for the tombola. Everyone contributes things they wanted to chuck out from the pantry, and some items have been doing the rounds for years. There's always a Rubik's cube and a bottle of ouzo someone's lost interest in. Some of the tinned items have sell-by dates back in the 1980s.

It's one thing after another: raffles, auctions, craft fayres, lucky dips, Secret Santas … All of them involve the redistribution of tat that no one really wants because everyone has been saving the bath salts and the dreary manicure set they were given for Christmas last year to put in the tombola for this Christmas. You can find yourself coming home with a 70s' fondue set that you won, and struggling to find somewhere to put it until *next* year's collection for the tombola.

I'm sorry, but the whole charity business leaves me cold. At the WI jumble sale you know that the woman with a scowl that could take out entire families at a glance has rummaged through all the stuff when she was putting it out and has nicked all the good cashmere and anything remotely worth having. Otherwise, why would she be running the stall again this year?

Of course, if you're really middle class (which I'm not), you do that whole charity Christmas thing. You spend Christmas Day running the centre for down and outs, and you exchange gifts that come only from charity shops with your family and loved ones. But if you do, and your family give you a Tyrolean Hat and a hideous orange jumper that has gone all bobbly through too many washes, you feel unloved and spend the day sobbing when no one is looking because you wanted someone to buy you a nice pair of earrings.

The worst thing about Christmas is the emotional turmoil and the guilt – I cry at carols and I'm a Jewish atheist; I squander all my money on luxuries and really half the world's got nothing and I'm meant to be a socialist; and then I cook and eat turkey and I'm meant to be a vegetarian. So I'm just upset the whole time.

Michele Hanson

CHRISTMAS CARD HELL

And then, inevitably, the Christmas cards start coming, and coming and coming and coming, filling up all the shelf space and are there in a big pile to read every morning. And you haven't sent yours yet!

The entire Christmas card operation clogs up your time well into the early hours: looking up people's addresses, remembering their children's names and writing cheery messages. Then you have to spend hours at the post office weighing things and buying strange denominations of stamps for Canada or some unpronounceable country in Africa where your godson is spending his gap year. And as if that wasn't enough, there are the 'bouncers' – dozens of cards from people you hadn't intended to send one to. And the buggers keep arriving, every day – filling up the house and cluttering up the place so that you can't dust anything, and ensuring that you have to send them one back next year. There is truly no end to it. Even the cute sparkly one from a friend's two-year-old gets on your nerves because it leaves glitter all over the carpet for ever more. Just please, can we all STOP IT?

Then there's that stupid habit of sending cards to people you see every day – someone you sit next to at work, or your neighbour. You buy great big boxes of them and only have to go and get more. Then people send you customised ones that show their holiday snaps, which are really a way of letting you know that they went to the Caribbean this year. They might as well say, 'I'm on a yacht and you're not', or 'I've been to Barbados and you haven't'. I chuck them out on principle.

Then there are round robins the thickness of a novel – pages and pages of drivel about the dreary things that have happened to people during the year, which I have no interest in whatsoever. Last year someone sent us one that more or less told us their bank balance: it listed all the houses they had bought and sold in one year. These missives go straight in the bin too. And the corporate company Christmas cards really take the biscuit.

You get Christmas cards from your building society – a crappy Christmas card with everybody's photocopied signatures. Do me a favour – just give me faster service when I come in and want some money. I don't want a bloody Christmas card.

Jane Moore

The cards from people are fine; the ones from organisations really piss me off. I get a card from the firm I once bought a sofabed from – Merry Christmas, Germaine! From all at Slumbersoft. I don't want Merry Christmas from all at Slumbersoft, thank you very much.

Germaine Greer

FUN AND FRIVOLITY

At school, on top of the charity tasks, there are all the Christmas activities that have to be organised and gone to. The inevitable nativity play or Christmas concert happens, and Miss sends home a great long list of things that need to be done for it. Hello? I thought you teachers were in charge of this, but no, they need a costume – medieval knight with feathered hat and velvet slippers, or an Afro-Caribbean peasant. It was bad enough when they were a fairy in the nativity play and you could just adapt their ballet costume, or a shepherd and you could send them in an old nightdress with a tea towel on their head. But oh no, all the perfect mothers are making proper costumes, including wings and headdresses. So there you are at two in the morning with the sewing machine and some pipe cleaners, wondering how to get your own back on Miss.

You have to get Granny along to the play, you have to take the afternoon off work, and you have to get a good seat because you must make sure you are seen by your little darling. Then they start singing 'Away in a Manger' and you cry so much you can't see a thing.

Even something as traditional as the nativity play is not without its stress – underneath the tea towels and tinsel lies the long hard lobby to get your child a decent part, like Mary or Joseph or the narrator. Winning the X-Factor would be easier.

Advent calendars have to go up on 1 December, so they have to be bought well in advance, and naturally they have to be the all-singing, all-dancing ones. It's no good buying something religious and glittery; they have to have chocolates in each window, and a CD in the last one at the very least. But you always get the wrong one. Last year they loved Barbie and Ken's calendar, so this year you buy the same and discover they want *Sex and the City*. You can't win.

Then some bright spark in the office decides to get all festive. Audrey gets out the Christmas decorations from the stationery cupboard – the cheapest, vilest silver paperchains that droop down from the ceiling. So not even work is a Christmas-free zone. Some of my sadder colleagues put a little Christmas tree on their own desk and Blu-Tack some cards at the back of them. Usually the woman on reception has the most, but then she sends a card to everyone. Audrey has taken bookings for the Christmas lunch back in March, so back in March you chose your starter, your main course and pud. It's in some ghastly hotel, and you are one of a party of 28. No one does a seating plan, so you are sitting with the most boring person in the office and can't hear yourself think above the din of the BT party at the table next door. Some people get very drunk indeed. Some people get frisky. You can't wait to get home, and promise yourself that next year you will save yourself £35 and the dreariest afternoon of the year.

The worst thing in the world is an office party – desperate, desperate, desperate. All these girls in outfits that are too tight, too low, too short, in shoes that don't fit, trying to hit if off with guys who they don't like. Men who are married with their tie loosened, drunk and dribbling, trying to squeeze some girl that they've been grinning at each year. Then you have the people with their trousers off trying to photocopy their body parts on the Xerox machine. No, no, no – desperate, desperate, desperate.

Jenni Trent Hughes

Either that or your office party is effectively a paper plate full of Twiglets at your desk with some sweet white wine or a sherry, and the phones ringing all around you. Then someone arrives with a sexy Santa outfit and makes you feel fat and forty.

What really annoys me at Christmas parties are those young women who dress up as sexy Santas or sexy elves – the combo of Christmas hat and a little red dress and then stockings. I can't be doing with that.
Jenny Eclair

There is nothing more depressing or disheartening than actually having a lot to do *at work* at Christmas. I have spent the two weeks running up to it simply trying to make myself heard on the phone against the din of 'Jingle Bells' and party tooters.

And everyone else seems to be having so much fun, there are endless articles in *Heat* and *Cosmopolitan* on the perfect party planner, or the perfect party outfit for the party season. And the only thing you have been invited to is the coffee morning at Tumble Tots, or the PTA disco. Wahey! People stumble into work with a hangover day after day, and you have been tucked up in bed each night after icing the Christmas cake until two in the morning.

CHRISTMAS SHOPPING

The kids' presents are obviously the ones you spend most time buying, and usually there is some God-awful rush on for the big craze of the moment. This means that not only are we trying to get all the things on the letter they sent to Santa, but we are also queuing up with hundreds of other parents at Toys R Us on a Saturday in December to get the latest delivery of Tracey Islands, Buzz Lightyears or whatever the latest craze from America is because the thought of your little darling being the only one in the playground without one of these wretched things is too hard to bear. You get one, usually, after putting in dozens of hours hunting on the Internet and then driving to Bicester where they've had a bumper delivery …

but by the time you get to Christmas Day, the kids have all moved on to something else and the 'latest craze' is now a bit passé.

If it were just shopping for presents, it wouldn't be so bad, but shopping for food is the other thing that keeps you busy for *months* in the run-up to Christmas. Delia's countdown dictates that the pudding and cake be made in October so that they mature properly. Delia makes all manner of marzipan and organic lovelinesses and gets them all sitting in rows, frozen and labelled ready for the big off. You plan to do all these things, *want* to do all these things, but one by one the deadlines come and go and the weeks tick by and you have to chuck in the towel and buy ones ready made off the shelf. This will be something that your mother-in-law will tut-tut about because in her day she did have time.

So one bleak early morning in the week before Christmas you go to Tesco's for one big almighty shop. You need two trolleys. *Two trolleys*. And you get there nice and early to beat the crowds. Think again. You turn up in the freezing cold, dark morning of 23 December like every other woman in the country. You get to the store at 7.45 a.m. and already the car park is full. Next year you'll bring a military tank to shove them all out of the way. The shop is full of women like you, who have had the idea of beating the crowds and getting it all done, getting in front, because you want to be relaxed and gorgeous and serene on Christmas Eve, like in the magazines, not shopping, so it's all got to be done now. You wait for the doors to open knowing that you will have to fight off the oppositions if there aren't enough organic turkeys go round.

Everyone starts doing the 'organic turkey trot' – you are trying to look like you are just walking but actually you are running. You know that

these women will fight you for the organic turkey with that steely
determination that comes with many years of hockey playing.
Jenny Eclair

Then, guess what? They've run out of mince pies, turkey
stuffing and anything else remotely Christmassy. You're left
staring at shelves of Easter eggs and a sign saying 'More
organised women than you have already bought all the
sprouts, so bog off'. The checkout queues are so long that they
curl round on themselves at the back of the store, so you have
to ask people to move out of your way to get to anything at all.
The empty shelves mean you've got to go to other shops for
the cranberry sauce and some sprouts. Because obviously
Christmas wouldn't be perfect without them.

Christmas Eve finally comes round, and everything is
wrapped and the food is under control. There are sides of cold
meat, mounds and mounds of vegetables, and every cupboard,
drawer and work surface is groaning with food.

Before the kids go to bed you can do all those marvellous
magical things, such as put the glass of sherry and carrot out
for Santa and the reindeer. Of course, now that the kids
'know' about Father Christmas, this ritual is for me more than
them, but still we go through it. Grumpy turns all the lights off
and we have to stumble around by candlelight, which is all
very romantic and gorgeous for about half an hour, then one
sets the wallpaper on fire, we spill some red wine over the rug
and it all goes horribly wrong. So there's about half an hour on
Christmas Eve when I think it's all magical and I get a bit
weepy, and then I am so knackered with all the preparation
that has driven me into the ground for the last three months
that I badly need to go to sleep. But of course the kids are so
whizzed up with excitement that you can never get the little
blighters in bed. You're desperate to do all the stuffing of the

stockings and pillowcases, and put the gold coins that Santa has 'dropped' all down the stairs and so on. I believed in Santa until I was embarrassingly old, into my first boyfriend more or less, but these days some snotty kid tells them at school when they're eight and it's all ruined far too soon.

As a child, I remember waking up on Christmas morning to find what Santa had brought me and thinking, 'Hey, how mean are my mum and dad? Santa buys me all this stuff, mounds and mounds of it, and all my mum and dad have got me is this lousy Tressy doll with hair that is supposed to grow and so does not. She just has a stupid hole in her head with some horrid hair you can roll out. Santa spent a fortune on me and I've only met him once, in his grotto.'

AT LAST …

Once Christmas Day itself arrives, the countdown turns into an hour-by-hour military operation.

0530

The alarm wakes you to put the turkey on and defrost the cocktail sausages. You get to the kitchen and the bird hasn't defrosted, so you put the hairdryer on it for half an hour. Bet it's not like this at Delia's.

You get the oven dish out for the turkey and remember that this time last year (almost to the minute) you had the same maddening problem of the turkey being too big for the tray, and (again) have to saw off one of the legs to get it in, there's still a bit hanging over the edge and so all the fat drips into the oven all morning, making horrid smoky smells and creating a job for you that will involve rubber gloves and some foamy substance that will create its own hole in the ozone layer above your house. It's all looking a bit like *The Texas Chainsaw Massacre*.

0620
Try to get back to sleep.

0621
One of the kids comes in saying, 'He's been.'

0700
All the Santa presents that took you two months to buy are now open.

0710
You put the day's first batch of rubbish in a bin bag.

0711
The kids watch some tosh on Sky TV about celebrities at Christmas, while you listen to some carols on Radio 4 and try

to be festive. Delia has piped her meringues by now, so you are already behind.

0800

You start peeling potatoes.

0830

Second bag of rubbish to the bin.

The kitchen is overrun with food. The fridge is full to bursting. You write out daily menus, like Delia. Everyone has a strict programme of when and what they have to eat. But then someone goes and opens a chocolate orange from their stocking and you're stuffed, or rather they're stuffed, and then the whole menu is put out. And all this time things are going off. All those sides of ham and smoked salmon that you bought are going past their sell-by dates – something more to worry you.

1130

Coffee and petits fours. Auntie Marjorie arrives and there's the presents to look forward to … and yet the presents destined for you under the tree are the ones that haven't even been wrapped – they're still in their M&S bags. You know they're not going to fit, so hope to goodness that the giver has saved the receipt. Your Grumpy Old Man long ago stopped buying you something romantic, but non-stick pans … I mean, really! He also gives you some CDs of Roy Orbison or the Beach Boys that he actually wants himself. Or some recipe books – oh, nice. Enough to make you want to rush out and buy yourself some soft porn.

With presents, size matters. The bigger the box, the more likely it is to be some hideous gadget from Dixons. The smaller the box, the more likely it is to be the all-important jewellery gift. We can hope. Even when Grumpy does buy me jewellery, he goes for what I can only describe as pendants – great big lumps of amber that probably cost a fortune but look a bit like the things that dangle round the necks of music teachers with breath that smells like cat litter.

One Christmas my husband gave me a chenille hand-knitted bobble hat. It was like we'd never met. I opened it and I said, 'Did you not like me when you bought me this?' and he said, 'I thought it would be really fun'. 'For who?' I wasn't even remotely gracious and my sister said, 'I can't believe how rude you are to him.' I replied, 'It's much better to be honest now. I've spent a lifetime pretending to like presents and I'm certainly not going to do it with my husband.'
Arabella Weir

Even your mother gets it wrong. You'd think someone in the family might find something to pamper you with, something devilishly stylish or simply to die for. Mothers can be even

worse than lovers – usually their presents have some subtext, some agenda, which is something like, 'Darling, you need to lose weight', or 'Darling, you need to be a better wife/better cook', or some other little hurtful message. My mother usually buys me some gripper knickers or some hideous nightdress that she's bought from a mail-order catalogue that's obviously aimed at people with a dress size that suits kaftans – usually with a nasty name like 'Little Secrets' or something really unpleasant like 'Larger Lovelies', which is just code for 'Stop raiding the biscuit tin or you'll be my size the day after tomorrow'. Mothers, who'd have 'em?

1230

The neighbours pop in for a drink and to bring you the whole Stilton, exactly like the one they bought you five years ago, and every year since, because you said you liked it so much. You hate Stilton. You also dread them popping round some time on Boxing Day saying they have run out of Stilton and could they possibly scrounge some back because the truth is that you wrap it up straight away and give it to the Kinsellas on Boxing Day morning because they really do like Stilton … or at least they *say* they do.

1330

The panic to get all the food ready and on the table at the same time.

My slightly menopausal mother with an electric carving knife – not a good combination. She'll be carving the turkey but looking at all of us. She could have gone for any one of us at any moment. And have you ever tried to get a turkey out of the oven? It's very heavy; it's a bit like getting a fat child out of a playpen. Really difficult to manoeuvre. A great big Pot Noodle in Christmas dinner flavour – put it in the middle of the table and give everyone a fork. Now that would be a great idea …

Jenny Eclair

1500

We all have to rush the end of Christmas lunch to watch the Queen. It's my mother who insists we watch because she keeps threatening it's going to be her last Christmas – my mum's, that is, not the Queen's. (I imagine they'll stuff the Queen for several years after she actually dies and just wheel her out at state occasions and put her in a big blue hat on the balcony.) The Queen's not had to do any Christmas shopping at all. Probably had a team of people sorting out the menus, organising seating arrangements, doing her hair and buffing up the corgis. She's had time for a nice windy walk in Balmoral followed by a pre-lunch sherry. What does she know about real life?

The older I get, the more bad tempered I become about the Royal Family. I think they're a waste of food and that we should all grow up and elect a president like every other nation. That way we can go and visit Buckingham Palace all year round and inspect the nation's treasures at our leisure, rather than form a queue round the block every August to get a glimpse – and be charged in the process. I enjoy it when they humiliate themselves, like on *It's a Royal Knockout* (which apparently can't even be shown on TV any more because it was so embarrassing) and when they have messy divorces and get into scuffles with photographers. But when they sit in an armchair, as the Queen does on Christmas Day, and pontificate about the Commonwealth and all that nonsense I feel like throwing something.

In fact, I get less and less tolerant of the upper classes as I get older too. They will set themselves apart, won't they? With their hacking jackets and revolting dogs, and stupid school uniforms with bow ties or silly hats or something else that tells us that they are paying a lot in school fees. And they have no self-doubt. Self-doubt doesn't really figure in their lives. They bark at you on the phone and say, 'D'you see?' after uttering the simplest of sentences. Well, yes, of course I see, you old fart. They claim never to watch the telly, especially anything common like *Corrie*, but I bet they watch it secretly in a little corner of their huge stately piles when no one else is looking. They sob and sob and say how badly they are missing their children who are away at school. Well, here's the thing; you don't *have* to send them off to boarding school, you know. Their children talk about dorm captains and dorm fun and generally behave in a way that makes you want to slap them.

1530

Once the Queen's speech is over, I get settled on the sofa for the first time in about three months and would rather like a snooze, but the house is a mess and the dog has been sick because it ate the leftover Christmas pudding (which is most of it, as per normal). No one has made even the slightest dent in the mountain of food that is making the fridge so full you can't actually find anything.

1600

The Barbie doll has shoes so small that you can barely see them with a naked eye, so you'll have to get some more the day after Boxing Day. The pogo stick has broken, the computer game doesn't fit our PC, but my non-stick pans are coming into good use. Junior Monopoly is out again, my mother has had too much to drink, the telly is a pile of shit and I don't even like Melberry fruits. Oh, good. Glad I spent so much of my life organising it. Next year I promise it's all going to be different. Yes, right.

I always imagine that Christmas is going to be relaxing. This is my dream, this is my goal. I imagine that once I get *this* list out of the way and everything's prepared, I can just glide serenely about the house with my hair done and some make-up on, or sit in front of the fire and just, well, chill. But it never seems to happen. I never seem to get the pinny off. All those movies I highlighted in the *Radio Times* come and go without me seeing any of them, and then when I do sit down there's nothing I want to see on the telly. I don't want *How Clean Is Your House at Christmas*, or *Christmas Property Ladder* or *Changing Rooms Christmas Special*. I want *It's a Wonderful Life*, or I want to sing along to 'Climb Every Mountain', but they always put these kinds of thing on at 1.45 in the afternoon when we're still having lunch.

I don't relax at any time of the year, so the idea is to relax at Christmas. But the only way you could have a stress-free Christmas if you've got a mother, a father, a husband, a child or a friend would be if you were in a coma.

Arabella Weir

Still next year it might not be your turn to do Christmas, and then you will be really understanding and helpful to the woman who is getting all hot and flustered in the kitchen. Not.

If somebody else lands the Christmas Day slot you know you are off the hook. You know that they're suffering but suddenly you become like their great-great-grandmother, feet up on the coffee table and, 'Oh yes, I'll have another brandy.' You know that you should have some Christmas spirit and go and help. But no, because you did it last year. So hah, they can suffer.

Kathryn Flett

1900

Party games. As in most households, it's a ritual. Charades and the pea-sucking game, where you have to kneel on the floor and by sucking through a straw transfer as many dried peas as you can from one bowl to another against the clock. When my mother plays she can never get back up from the floor, which is always the thing that most amuses the kids over Christmas.

Party games are one thing most grumpy old women seem to like at Christmas. It's a way of getting their own back – thrashing the kids or, even better, their husbands, at a game of Old Maid or Pictionary. The teenagers look super fed-up and as if they can't wait to get back to their hair straightening or their dance mats, but we like to think we can make our own entertainment, thank you very much.

In some ways the only way round the repetitive strain injury of Christmas is to spend it alone. I usually feel sorry for my friends who do that year after year, and ask whether they want to join us for lunch or drinks, but I think they might have hit on the answer. A soak in the bath, some scented candles, a (half) bottle of champagne and a turkey dinner for one. No leftovers, and all the flatulence, nose-picking and gluttony you could imagine. You wouldn't need to get dressed at all; you wouldn't have any washing up because you'd just eat it all out of the cartons. You'd flick from channel to channel on the TV all day and all evening, doing just what you wanted. You wouldn't have to see any family. And you wouldn't have to write any thank-you notes. I can see the appeal, except some do-gooder from the church would probably pop round for a cheer-up chat, assuming you were near suicide or something. That would ruin it.

COME-DOWN

Once Christmas Day is over, there's the taking-back list. These joyous errands always fall into women's in-tray – hours and hours of queuing at the specially made queue barriers at M&S, with items that are already in the sales.

Then there's a bit of normality between Christmas and New Year, where I can generally let my hair down for a few days. Nothing much is happening, there are no visitors, there's still a mountain of food to eat, but the kids are nice and preoccupied with their new toys, and I might manage an afternoon of not doing too much.

Then New Year looms, and it goes without saying that I don't go to cool all-night drinking raves. In fact, if I'm honest, I never have been invited to a really cool New Year party. When I was a kid I was thrilled enough to stay up late and watch Andy Stewart and Moira Anderson in their kilts in a dreary black and white studio. Val Doonican probably did a big number at midnight, then I went to bed feeling very grown up indeed. But now everyone else seems to be having such a lovely time at New Year parties, falling about with party tooters and snogging all and sundry.

Once January comes round, you take the kids to see *Jack and the Beanstalk*, starring someone who was once in *EastEnders*, or Jordan's sister, or a Krankie or two. It starts with a group scene of all the cast, plus a few amateurs milling about pretending to be part of a street scene in medieval London, and from then on the plot just gets worse. Is there a plot? You know the baddies and the goodies because for some reason the people in the front row know when to boo and when to cheer, but the show is really only an excuse to see Frank Carson's end-of-pier summer routine in bobble hats. I truly, truly hate pantomimes. I can't tell you how bored I get, and then the kids ask me something about the plot and I have absolutely no idea because I just drift off into my own daydream. Except I do know when the interval is and how long there is to go. And I know that without even looking at my watch.

It's no wonder you're pleased to be back at work, pleased to be writing some new lists for the new year in your nice clean diary. And it all cost a mere £800 ...

CHAPTER NINE

Children and animals

CHILDREN ARE QUITE SIMPLY IN CHARGE THESE DAYS. Mothers in supermarkets say pathetic things like, 'Now I'm going to count to three and you have to put that ice cream back in the freezer, or Mummy's going to be very annoyed … one, two, two and a half, two and three quarters' … they're still counting half an hour later. 'Mummy will be very annoyed.' Scar-ee. Mummy'll give you a clip round the ear or stop you watching *The Simpsons* for a week – now that's more like it.

And parents seem to think they have to explain the *logic* of everything to their little darlings: the *logic* of not being rude to people, the *logic* of not spitting out your baked beans at someone, the *logic* of not throwing your beaker at the lady on the till … Just stop him doing it … now. Stop him yelling and shouting and screaming while I am trying to enjoy a bit of 'me' time. And why do we now have to keep children amused all the time? Why can't they sometimes be told just to sit still and shut up for a while? Why do we all have to spend all our time amusing or stimulating the children with educationally sound toys, or cutting and sticking sessions, or some such nonsense. And whose idea was glitter glue? Honestly …

Children aren't *ready* to know the ins and outs of

everything – about the political regime in the Sudan, or the world economy, or the green pound. Sometimes they need to be told to do things because you say so, or that they can't do something because no means no.

Having said that, I think my parents went a bit too far the other way. They told me that the cute little sheep I saw with their heads sticking out of the cattle trucks on the motorway were 'going on their holidays', and I believed them until I was about 16. I couldn't understand why vegetarians were so bothered about us eating meat: surely the animals were dead anyway? (My parents had also edited out the bit about us actually killing them on purpose.) As a result, adulthood hit hard.

My parents didn't worry too much about keeping me amused. I was bored for my entire childhood. *Blue Peter* was the highlight of my week; *Bleep and Booster* was a really big deal for me. These days we all have to make sure the children are busy and stimulated all day, every day, with tae kwon do, or cello lessons, or chess championships, and Duke of Edinburgh awards … Seven days a week, 24/7, as we have to say now.

Children's lives now – every single nanosecond has to be accounted for. When I was a kid I seem to remember that eight hours a day was spent sleeping, and 16 hours a day was spent being incredibly bored, waiting for something interesting to happen.

Kathryn Flett

Sundays when I was little were boredom itself. Nothing to do except Sunday school, and then *Two-way Family Favourites* with Jean Metcalfe and Cliff Michelmore, your pogo stick to play on and a packet of Spangles if you were lucky. A bit of Plasticine and some join-the-dots was as stimulating as it got, and then you'd put on your roller skates with the extendable metal bits that didn't work very well, and kill some time skating round the cul-de-sac. *Songs of Praise* or *Sing Something Simple* came on, and you were pleased, actually pleased, to hear them because it meant that Sunday was nearly over and school was the next morning. Of course you weren't allowed to stay up to watch *Up Pompeii* – not that you would have understood it anyway. Bad or what?

Actually, I think children should be taught to be bored. I was in a coma of boredom throughout the 70s. The shops weren't even open on a Sunday, and your nana, both your nanas, came for lunch and you had to be there.

Jenny Eclair

Of course, now that my biological clock has stopped ticking and I am extremely unlikely to procreate again, the whole business of motherhood, young toddlers and babies bores me rigid. It was interesting when it was happening to me. It's not interesting when other people are doing it. Young mothers go on and on about their NCT classes or their funny stretch marks, or their post-natal classes and their pelvic floor exercises and they just make me fed up. Yes, we've all been there, yeah, childbirth hurts like hell. Get over it.

Even when my own children were small and I had to feed what seemed like the entire street with fish fingers and oven chips of an evening, I found it hard to be nice to other people's children. I mean, yes, of course I am nice to other people's children – what do you take me for? But you do need a spot of patience to scrape up all that tomato ketchup and wipe down the high chairs and hose down the cupboards after every meal, and when they're not yours it is extremely difficult to keep the lid on your impatience. So now that the kids are much older, and small children do not feature in my life on a daily basis, when I do bump into them on buses or in shops they really do just get on my nerves, I'm afraid. Sorry and all that, but they do.

The buggies have got bigger, the amount of paraphernalia has tripled, and it's no good opening a jar of meat and potato gunge – they have to have organic, genetically sound ranges of baby food flown in from Zanzibar. They need flashcards presented to them at 20-minute intervals all night because someone wrote an article claiming that if you do that for the first two years of babies' lives, they are more likely to get a place at Oxford, or some such nonsense.

Baby's nursery has to be colour coordinated, with Ahlberg posters on the wall and gorgeous linen sheets on the cot, with some fragrant real nappies because now disposables are so 'white trash', and some home-made mobiles. Now you have to let the baby cry, let it feed when it wants to, and let it walk all over your family life. In other words, generally be at its beck and call day and night. People will come round to supper and baby will be centre stage. Some women go on breastfeeding these days until baby is around 18 months old, even though by then baby will be able to sit up and grin at everyone between suckles, with a bit of milk trickling out of its mouth to embarrass everyone. All this, they say, is 'best for baby'.

Educationally sound toys fill the nursery, as well as the living room, spare room and kitchen. Mother and toddler groups, tumble tots, playgroups, play mornings and all manner of dull and dreary groups of women will get together to make sure that baby is stimulated at all times. You can't leave your buggy outside shops any more, so it gets pushed round everywhere, snagging people's heels and ankles and tripping us all up. Some of them are the size of those little electric cars – big enough to get a parking ticket.

People are so obsessed with their offspring that they put stickers on the back of their cars saying 'Baby on Board' or, as I saw recently, 'Twins On Board'. Unlike most people, I rather like these signs, but I think there should be more of them with more information. I think there should be ones that say, 'Spoilt Brats on Board', 'Minor Celebrity on Board', 'Someone Who Was on Big Brother on Board', 'Britney Spears Lookalike on Board' … that way I can choose who I ram the back of. So if it said Brian Sewell or Eminem, we could all club together and form an organised attack.

PARTY TIME

Children's social lives are a squillion times better than mine. Parties, sleepovers, playdates – I don't remember doing any of that. I remember the odd fancy dress party with pass-the-parcel and a sponge cake with some candles, but these days organising your child's birthday is like planning a wedding. Youngest Daughter starts to talk about hers in January, and her birthday is in November. Invitations, pick-up times, cinema trips, stretch limos, children's entertainers, themed teas, endless party games with endless prizes and presents, treasure hunts, jugglers, party tooters and the inevitable party bags. Party bags were always the bit about the children's parties that gave me the most stress. I'd be laying them all out for a week beforehand, collecting affordable cute little girly trinkets and things that you can buy 20 of without breaking the bank. Then the little brats would turn up their noses at the balloons or the mini Aero bars I put in there for padding. 'Are there any, like, presents in the party bags?' they'd say. Or 'I've already got a hair bobble like this at home,' or 'At Amanda's we got Chanel.' Well, tough.

Children's parties are a steep learning curve. I made some horrible mistakes with the first few. When we started, I assumed that children were like adults at parties – relatively well behaved, relatively easy to please. *Wrong.* I put on the invites 3.00 – 7.00 p.m. – four hours I reckoned was about right, what with all the games, the treasure hunt, the tea and musical statues and the like. What I hadn't appreciated is that by 3.15 there are 15 kids running up and down the stairs, three boys sliding down the banister and one girl in tears. Only my mother is the least bit interested in stick the tail on the donkey. Indeed, the children scoff in disgust when you suggest it. You bring tea forward as a way to get them all in one room: the Ribena is spilt, the chocolate cake crumbles and gets trodden all over the house, and by 5.30 you are desperate for the parents to come and collect, but still have an hour and a half of it. No wonder the parents all dropped off the kids and left with a spring in their step after checking the pick-up time – like they were off on a short weekend break; never known so much free time on a Saturday. Other, more sensible mothers rent the village hall, put some sausages on sticks, play a few disco records and that's that. But because I was a working mum and because it all had to be perfect, the two girls' birthdays kept me busy for a third of the year.

You can't even get them a bog-standard sponge cake with some candles: it has to be a personalised cake, with themes based on their current obsession, such as swimming pools or ponies or the Woodcraft Folk. You have to book a DJ to do spot prizes and bring some dry ice. In my day you got a plate of Twiglets and some pineapple and cheese on a stick and, if you were lucky, a balloon to take home (that you had to blow up yourself). A balloon. That's one balloon.

And while we're on the subject of cakes ... I'll kill Jane Asher. The one and only time I ever attempted a full-on 'concept' cake for Youngest Daughter, the whole debacle effectively shortened my life. I'm not good at making cakes, so I go for one of Jane's 'easy concepts', as she puts it in the picture. I get the scales and weigh out all the ingredients, as Jane does in little white dishes, and feel, for a couple of minutes, like a domestic goddess. Then, inevitably, I cut a few corners and stick the eggs in too fast, so that they curdle, and then I have to put in more flour than I'm supposed to. Jane takes lots of things for granted: like she thinks you know how to manipulate greaseproof paper to go around those infuriating corners of cake tins, and that you know how much cold water is needed to make the right consistency. Wrong. I do not know. More flour, and then more eggs than in the recipe and it had started to look like pizza dough, not cake mixture.

After half an hour cleaning the kitchen while the mixture's in the oven, you try it and it doesn't seem to be cooking. You prod and poke about and it's still runny inside, and eventually you take it out. Jane doesn't say whether you are supposed to turn the thing out of the cake tin instantly or wait for it to cool, so I plump for tipping it out straight away. But because it's risen in the middle into such a pointy mound, the thing is aerodynamically unstable, so it starts to break up in front of my eyes. I prop it up with cookery books and saucepans, hoping to halt the process, but to no avail.

After a couple of calls to friends and another trip to Tesco's for some marzipan and another jar of raspberry jam, I am persuaded to switch concept and go to page 36 – the Pirate Cake with the fluffy icing and gold coins all round the edges. This means a trip to Woolworth's for gold-wrapped chocolate coins. They had none. They'll be getting them again at Christmas. Oh, good.

I tip the icing sugar into a bowl and a cloud fills the kitchen, making me cough and wheeze, and covering the whole room with a fine layer of sugar dust – like the one we had for a month when the builders were knocking through the pantry. I put the mixer in at full throttle. Now the kitchen is splattered in icing blobs that have flicked all over the window and the work surface and inside the open cutlery drawer, necessitating all the things inside the drawer to be removed, washed and dried. Oh, really … I throw Jane Asher's book on the floor and jump on it in a fit of temper like a four-year-old, then go out for some fresh air to calm down.

By the time I calm down, the icing has dried – not in perfect fluffy peaks, but in runnels over the plate and on to the kitchen table.

The sheer bulk of it meant I had to put it on the bird table in two stages. I can't really say that the birds enjoyed it. I hoped the rain would wash it away. Gosh, wasn't there a song about that once?

I just wish there wasn't so much pressure to be domestic
goddesses on top of everything else. There's bloody Delia and
Nigella managing to serve up all sorts of deliciousness, and
you feel that you should be doing the same. When my mother
was keeping house and home, cooking was altogether much
simpler – steak and kidney pie with mash, or roast chicken
with gravy. Leftovers on Monday, baked beans on toast
Tuesday. Baked potatoes were positively exotic, olive oil in
those days was something you put in your ears if you had
earache, and before Fanny and Johnny Cradock you'd never
heard of duck à l'orange. You put lard on your suntan, and
Vesta curry mix was cause for big celebration. Now you're
expected to knock up home-made pesto sauce, make your
own chapatti bread, mix your own curry powders and
marinate your own laundry. And that's just in the week.
When you've got people coming round to dinner you need to

be stone-grounding the basil and home-growing the asparagus
for the starter alone. You read *Prima* or *Good Housekeeping*, and if
you go out to work you feel you really should be baking your
own bread. Keeping up with Nigella. So you buy a breadmaker
that is so complicated it has a manual as thick as the phone
book, and it takes so long to fiddle about with it that you use it
only four times, which works out at about £15 a loaf. Rather
heavy loaves at that. Then it clutters up your kitchen and
makes you feel annoyed. The same can be said for pasta
machines and ice-cream makers. Anyone who buys you one
for your birthday should be deleted from your contacts book
or divorced. Furthermore, unused kitchen gadgets that gather
dust on the work surface also underline for all to see your
failure to be a good, wholesome mother.

FURRY FRIENDS

The need to provide your children with a perfect childhood is
overwhelming – I'm sure much more pressing than it was to
my parents. Is it because women work so hard? Is it because
women have so many more demands on their time? But we all
feel we are slaves to our children and their childhoods. They
want a pet badly enough, then we feel that for their emotional
development they need a pet. As a child I longed for a dog like
Blue Peter's Shep or Petra, but the most my parents would put
up with was a tortoise that went up in the loft in a shoebox for
the entire winter and was dull as dishwater the rest of the year.
My parents weren't stupid. Who wants to be cleaning out
hamster cages? And a trail of sawdust in the house is no
woman's idea of fun. I've lost count of how many pets my
daughters have persuaded us to have when they were in their
puppies and ponies years, which seemed to last for a very long
time indeed. It doesn't help that people keep writing hundred

of kids books, such as *Puppy Patrol, Jess the Border Collie, Hamster up a Drainpipe* and other such dross. And if you are clever enough to refuse to get a puppy, and a pony is out of the question, this leaves you with rabbits and rodents.

When I first gave in to pets we went into the pet shop and I asked the spotty assistant with a body odour problem what he thought would make good pets for a five-year-old and a nine-year-old. He persuaded me that the best pets by far would be rats. Must have seen me coming. He said they were the most intelligent creatures, and made ideal pets for small children. And they only cost £1.80 each. The girls put their pocket money on the counter in a flash. You have to buy two – obviously – so that they don't get lonely, then you go round the store and collect up all the paraphernalia that you'll need to go with the livestock … there's the cage, nesting, sawdust, food, water containers, and then all the things to amuse them, such as roundabouts, big dippers and tubes – their very own adventure park (because – like children – we mustn't let the rats get bored). The whole thing eventually came to about £160.

What Spotty Face in the pet shop didn't tell me was that rats, being very intelligent, are the cleverest escapologists imaginable. We had to take the entire bedroom apart on the first day, because one of them had gone missing and was found burrowing into the mattress. Eventually we had to take a Stanley knife to it. The pair went missing about once a week. They took to hiding behind the radiators, and after a while, rather than tip the entire contents of a room upside down, we went round the house looking for their horrid tails dangling down behind them keeping warm. Not that I could ever pick them up, or only with rubber gloves and a pair of kitchen tongs. Horrid little things. I never dared tell my mother they were on the loose in the house. She'd have had one of her turns.

Eventually they were put in the garden shed when the girls lost the first flush of interest in them, and there the sawdust doesn't bother you too much. Then one of the little darlings managed to eat its way out of the shed and into the gap between the shed and the garden wall. Grumpy and I had to take it in shifts to sit on a deckchair at the end of the gap waiting for the little bugger to come out. We baited it with all sorts of things – food, bits of chocolate and cheese, and sat there with a net through rain and shine for hours on end ready to catch it for our sobbing girls, who were afraid it might be too cold or too lonely. Eventually we flushed the little scamp out with the hosepipe and got it back into captivity. The girls then totally lost interest, as they do, and one of the rats managed to get up into the loft, where it gorged itself to death on the Christmas decorations – which didn't half give me a shock. I nearly fell off the stepladder when I found it the week before Christmas.

Pets are a bit like drugs: once you've done rats, you need to graduate up the food chain – hamsters, gerbils and eventually rabbits, cats and dogs. So we gave in to gerbils next. New cages and adventure parks – obviously – then the inevitable happens. You come down one morning and there are 11 gerbils where there were just two 'female' ones the night before. The girls started breeding gerbils and selling them to the pet shop, which I thought at first was a marvellous example of free enterprise. At one point we had a dormitory arrangement in the garden shed with cages of gerbils at all stages of their development. Then I noticed the girls decorating one of the cages with flowers and pieces of netting and ribbons, and was told it was the 'wedding cage'. Apparently the gerbils they wanted to mate were 'married' in a special ceremony, then put into the 'honeymoon' cage, where the two of them (and sometimes their friends) would watch the 'honeymoon' taking place.

Yes, you guessed it. Their way of finding out what the reproductive process looked like. Gerbil porn.

We live in deepest Northumberland, so one day the girls had the bright idea of getting a couple of pet lambs. I met a local farmer at a drinks party, and hey presto, we came home with pet lambs – orphans that had lost their mother in childbirth and needed bottle feeding. The farmer couldn't give them away quickly enough. First, I had to go off to the farmer's shop to get bottles and milk, which is an education in itself. The place is full of hideous things, such as plungers to help cows in labour, and torture-like clasps and harnesses for all sorts of things that I don't want to know about. There's also a lot of rat poison (if only I had known about this place when the two pet rats were around). The lamb's milk comes in bags the size of coal sacks, and the bottles are enormous – the girls had trouble carrying them. So guess who was mixing up lamb's milk and sterilising feeding bottles? Just the kind of extra job you need at six in the morning, and it stinks, it really stinks of rancid milk. Still, the first two mornings are a joy: you take some photos, get the video camera out, and the girls frolic around with them amongst the daffodils; but by the third morning you have to remind them to feed them, and by the fourth morning you do it yourself. It's worse than babies. Not only do they need feeding three times a day at regular intervals, but you have to go out into the garden shed in your dressing gown and a pair of wellies in the perishing cold to do it.

By about day ten I had a serious sense of humour failure, and instead of going out to give them their feed before bed, I decided to bog off down the pub with Grumpy. We came back a bit tipsy, struggled into the garden shed to feed the lambs, but they'd gone. Just a gaping door that they'd managed to push open – presumably out of hunger. The children were tucked up in bed and none the wiser, so out we went with torches, shouting, 'Lamby, lamby' among hundreds of other lambs in the fields with their mothers. Imagining the children's wretched faces the next morning, we even considered nicking a couple. We searched everywhere and then, at about two in the morning, Grumpy went to one more field up the road, taking a torch and the lambs' bottles to attract their attention. He heard their little bells in the distance, so he picked them up and put them in the car, making a terrible mess of the back seat, but the lambs were back safe and sound. All very lovely. Except that lambs turn into sheep. Within months. Bloody great sheep with huge bits of poo matted in their bottoms and hanging off their coats. Sheep don't want to play or have ribbons put round their neck or pose for photos. The girls naturally lost interest, and in the end we sent them home to the farmers 'for their holidays' and had our own *Born Free*-type ceremony. I didn't ask any tricky questions that I didn't want to know the answer to.

Next step up the food chain and you get a cat, because it's one step closer to the long-wanted puppy.

Cats are about as good as pets get, which is not very good in my book. You only need to chuck them some Whiskas and they get on with life. Not that they give a monkey's about anything or anyone. You can't sit them on your lap, and they don't like you fussing and stroking them. And they certainly don't like being dressed up in dolls' clothes and pulled around in prams, which is what the girls had in mind.

Cats don't give a shit, cats come and be fed and then they bugger off again, showing their bottom, which is really not nice. They don't poo outside; they poo inside the house in those tray things that single women then go and lovingly empty. Maybe it's the single equivalent of changing a nappy, but it doesn't do it for me.

India Knight

Inevitably the puppy pressure increases. The girls campaigned so hard – raised money to buy one doing all sorts of shows in the front room, as well as selling us back our own choc ices in the interval. There were poster campaigns all over the house, begging letters in my briefcase. So we gave in. Everyone signs an agreement about who is going to do what on which day, the walk rota is agreed and signed, so off you go to choose one. Bringing puppy home on their laps is the biggest day of their lives. They love their puppy. For a few months even. But steaming piles of whoopsie in the pantry and puppy training is no fun, and guess who gets on their knees to clear that lot up? Puppy training classes are something else. The woman we went to ran them from a caravan in her back garden, full of puppy treats and trophy cups and little girls spending their pocket money on trinkets for their beloved puppies. She was a bit gender unspecific, and the caravan stank of Capstan Full Strength, but she was doing a public service here – teaching dogs to poo outside instead of in the front room. Hours and hours were spent driving to this place, and our Saturday mornings were devoted to her classes.

You thought gerbils or rats were a nuisance, but at least they were mostly in a cage. My worst puppy experience (and there were many) was when I went to pick up a new car from the garage. A brand new lovely car, with spotless upholstery and gorgeous beige seats. I transferred all the supermarket shop to the back seat, and put puppy in the back with it. I was only going about a mile up the road, so off I went. I was halfway up the hill to our house when the puppy started to get a bit agitated in the back seat. I could sense it moving around, but I had a queue of traffic behind me, so I couldn't pull over. Then I saw the telltale going round in a circle movement in the rear view mirror and yes, the inevitable happened: puppy did a whoopsie on the spanking new back seat. They don't write cute puppy books about that. That wouldn't have been so bad, but then when I *did* stop, the puppy greeted me enthusiastically, as if she had never seen me before in her life – as dogs do – and bounded up and down and round over the whole thing, spreading dog poo all over the shopping, and all over the rest of the seats and floor. I spent a good hour and a half disposing of shopping, hosing down bits that could be salvaged, and putting air freshener and carpet cleaner all over the car. I didn't ever dare tell Grumpy. He didn't want the puppy in the first place. He often commented that the car didn't smell as nice as other new cars we've had. And where are the kids when this sort of catastrophe happens? They're at school, that's where.

And dogs simply poo so much. Before I had a dog I assumed they kind of did one once a day, like humans. But in fact every time you feed them they do a poo. And in the case of our dog – a Labrador – a poo the likes of which I'd go and see the doctor about if I did one. And dogs are about a quarter the size of humans. If you feed them twice a day, they do a poo that size twice a day. If you feed them three times a day, they produce three of them. Three of them to pick up and put in your anorak pocket, three of them to scrape off the back lawn, three of them to put in the dustbin. I am only going into this sort of detail because there may be someone reading this book who is thinking of getting a dog. Think again.

My sister's got this very bad dog called Charlie. When he drops a load, she puts an old Sainsbury's plastic bag on her hand, then she bends down and picks up the shit. She puts the bag into another plastic bag, and then she puts it in her anorak pocket. I swear blind that she forgets to take the dog shit bag out of her pocket. She might not wear that anorak for another three weeks, but then what has she got in that pocket? She's got three-week-old dog shit in her pocket, that's what.

Jenny Eclair

There is quite simply a need for dog toilets, with flushes and loo roll and a lock on the door.

When I go to my local park there are all these women walking around with terrible reversed plastic bags, and they pick up the poo, and very often, if the bag is leaky or something, they leave it by a lamppost, or there's a terrible bin, which I wouldn't dare look inside, which is the dog-poo bin. Imagine the poor person who has to empty that. I mean, that shouldn't be anybody's job, should it?

Sheila Hancock

The other big drawback with dogs is that they live a great deal longer than gerbils do, so you are still walking them when the kids are long gone to university. They all bog off and there you are still sending them newsy emails about how Lady is getting on, which they no longer have any interest in whatsoever.

Then there's all the pet deaths that have to be dealt with. Our garden is full of little mounds of dead gerbils, hamsters and rabbits, with crosses and home-made headstones. I think the girls shed more tears over losing the goldfish than they did about burying grandpa, and sometimes it's as well that they don't know that the cat ate the goldfish, or that the dog has started to dig up the hamster that you buried with them at the weekend and put up a darling little cross with IN LOVING MEMORY OF HAMMY written on it. Because one pet eating another is a hard lesson to learn.

CHAPTER TEN

A day in the life of ...

I'VE GOT ONE OR TWO THINGS OFF MY CHEST in the last few chapters, but if by any chance you have decided that I am just a bitch-madam-on-heat who deserves a big smack, well you might be right, but so far you have had only a *glimpse* of how terribly annoying I find everything, how very, very irritating the whole business of being me actually is. So I've decided to share with you some of the commonplace niggles of a typical day. Nothing fancy, nothing particularly stressful or unusual because that would be cheating. Just to give you some idea of the entire scale of the nark that I get myself into day in, day out.

When the alarm goes off at 6.30 in the morning, I'm usually already awake because now that I am officially old I am incapable of sleeping soundly. Someone 'mature' once said that their advice to the young was to get as much sex as possible while you can. Well, my advice would be to get as much sleep as possible while you can. I thought you were supposed to need less as you got older, so in that respect I am not yet old. It's not exactly worry that stops me sleeping – that happens during the day – it's more that now I'm older I take much longer to process everything. What did he mean when

he sent me that email? Why did she give me that look at
the hairdressers? It all festers and hangs about like a blocked
drain in my head and gets in the way of just, well, clearing it
all out.

The other thing that keeps me awake is my stupid
electronic personal organiser, on which I spent £500 of my
hard-earned money, and an entire day working out how to use
the thing and program it. When I say an entire day, I mean an
entire day. It's one of those raspberries or blackberries or
blueberries, and for the last week it has started ringing its
alarm thing in the middle of the night – not just a little alarm,
but one that wakes me up from downstairs in the hall. It goes
off for about a minute, then stops, and just as I start to drift off
to sleep again, it goes off again. This happens at ten-minute
intervals, until I get out of bed, put the lights on and go
downstairs to turn the wretched thing off. Then I realise that
I can't see it without my reading glasses on, so have to go back
upstairs, then down again with my specs, and eventually, when
I open it up, I realise it is trying to tell me that Auntie Doreen's
birthday is in three days' time. Or that the Derbyshires are
coming to supper in a fortnight. All the reminders and
anniversaries and birthdays I programmed in are sounding an
alarm at three in the morning, rather than at three in the
afternoon. It's just another example of technology being really
spiteful. Even when I turn it off completely in the middle of
the night, it still carries on, which is very comforting because
if we were to suffer a nuclear attack and I was in a bunker
somewhere, it would still be able to tell me when Uncle Billy's
birthday is. Trouble is, I have now thrown away the National
Trust calendar with all my handwritten birthday reminders, so
it would mean ringing round the entire family to find them all
out again. This means I have to live with the stupid piece of
high tech waking me up every few nights. Either that, or I have

to look at the manual or get in the telephone helpline queue. So obviously I choose it waking me up.

Technology means that there is simply so much more to go wrong. And so much more nannying and effort required from us to sort it all out. Now you have a 24-hour clock with seven different time zones on your alarm, whereas before you had a clock with a bell and lever at the top. Even when you stay in a hotel, it takes you half an hour to work out how to set it, then it wakes you up at three in the morning. I just want to call reception and ask them to do it, please.

WAKING UP

The alarm comes on to the *Today* programme because that's what middle-aged people like me are supposed to listen to. It washes over me like a bad headache – political story after political story which, frankly, I'm not that interested in; and if it's foreign news, I've lost the plot before it starts. I know that's a terrible thing to admit, but I do not read the overseas news pages in the *Guardian* from cover to cover every day. I read the *Daily Mail* and go straight to 'Femail' or the telly page to see what's on later. I can't be doing with Sarah Montague and John Humphreys showing off as if they're in the sixth form common room, and being so aggressive with politicians that I actually feel sorry for them. Their cohort James Naughtie will corner some minister and the conversation will go something like this (except it will go on in the same vein for about ten times as long):

> 'Yes, but did you know about clause 22b?'
> 'Well, I don't remember. I can't be expected to remember everything that comes through my office in two years of admin.'

'But Minister, did you know about clause 22b? It's a simple question and I think we are entitled to a simple answer.'

Oh, bog off and get on with something important, the two of you. The minister can't remember, and really, James, it is only you and John Humphreys and the newspaper editors who have to fill another paper tomorrow who care at all. Anyway, why can't the politician say, 'Look, I made a mistake, I goofed, or I just forgot. You try being minister for education one day, then minister for transport the week after because of a reshuffle.' No wonder politicians aren't really able to tell us anything truthful. When Paxman gets them in a muddle they always use that smokescreen phrase, 'Let's be really clear about this,' which is code for 'I don't really know what I think or what I should say, but it'll make me sound as if I do.'

Politics these days is just another soap, but without the glamour or the orthodontistry. Every night there's Andrew Marr or John Pienaar standing in front of Number 10 or having been dragged over to Washington LIVE (because everything has to be live) to tell us the political subtext of every story, which is code for the soap bit. I just watch and think, 'Poor sod' or 'He must be cold – look at that overcoat' or I wonder, 'Has he been sitting in the pub all evening waiting to do his bit? And what about his poor family never seeing him?' Or 'Nice tie' or 'Gosh, he's put some weight on.' I don't really listen to any of it. Then once in a while something happens, like we discover that Edwina Currie and John Major were at it over the desks late at night and I think, 'Now look, if you're going to be turning this into a soap, then go the whole hog. Let's have some cameras in the bar at Westminster so we can see who's flirting with whom, make our own guesses as to who might be having an affair.' That's more like it.

GETTING READY

Down in the kitchen, my routine starts. At my age I like a routine, so I start with black Earl Grey, and while I'm on the first mug, I make packed lunches. I am so fussy now that my tea even has to be in the right sort of mug. I don't like those tall, narrow mugs that mean the tea stays as hot as the Earth's core for hours on end; I like the big wide ones that mean you can get it down you sharpish. I put some fresh fruit in the packed lunches that I know will come back at the end of the day uneaten, but it makes me feel better. I first *find*, then iron sports kit, and in the rush I manage to singe the label on the front of the sweatshirt so it goes crusty and scratchy. I bag up spending money for school trips or subs for clubs. I then look at my line of satchels, errand bags, workbags and gym bags lined up by the front door and feel I am on top of the muddle – just for half an hour or so.

I usually manage to have a healthy breakfast because naturally I start every day meaning to be on a strict diet, and can usually continue this until about 10.30. I'm either on the low-fat or high-fat diet, the low-carb or high-carb, the GI or IG, the high-fibre or low-fibre – depending on the last article I read in a magazine. As the day goes on, the diet starts to unravel as people offer me chocolate biscuits, or my resolve weakens, and by 10 p.m. I am on the white wine and the Pringles. On a bad day I am on the kids' chocolate. So at Christmas the chocolate coins get bought about four times, and only the ones that I haven't eaten on Christmas Eve get scattered down the stairs as if dropped out of Santa's sack.

The thing that takes me longest in the morning – if I'm going out to work – is finding something to wear. You'd think that by my age I would know what I like, what colours suit me, and would have a wardrobe of coordinating separates hung up in colour order, but I start with the blue skirt and then can't find a blue top that doesn't make me look too fat. I can find dozens of black tops but no blue ones. You'd also think with all the Trinny and Susannah I watch that I'd have got the hang of buying outfits that match or coordinate by now. But I always seem to have the perfect wardrobe bar one pair of brown shoes, or one pink top – so I decide that once I buy that, everything will match with everything else, like a missing piece in a jigsaw. But then, when I buy it, I find I'm still missing something else. Other women seem to have it sussed; other women seem to look well turned out and colour coordinated every day of the week, with carefully chosen separates and cleverly knotted scarves that look sophisticated, whereas when I tie a scarf round my neck it just looks like I've got a sore throat.

Putting my tights on gets me very angry. One-size tights is a big lie. Either they're so small that the crotch rides down to your knees by 9 a.m. and you are walking around as if you have pooped your pants, or they are so big that they hang in folds all down your legs like Nora Batty's. And half the time I ladder them in the process of putting them on for the first time, which is just plain maddening.

Then my hair starts misbehaving. Normally I blow-dry my hair and have time to do only one half, so I look like I have been lying on my side in a wind-tunnel. I think hairdressers are taught to do special cuts that mean they look neat and lovely in the salon, especially in the rear-view mirror that they bring out with such aplomb, but once you blow-dry it yourself, the cut's designed to do something totally asymmetric so that you can never get it to look decent. That way you go running to them with more money for them to dry it for you for any special occasion. Again, I have spent my entire life growing my hair, then get to the stage where I'm bored with it, or my

hairdresser says it would look fab short, so I have it cut and
spend another six years growing out all the layers again.
Will I never learn?

I remind the kids to feed the dog and cat, and tell them
who is picking them up tonight and where. I have my usual
mad scramble to find some papers for work, which I've left
somewhere really obvious – well, it was obvious when I put
them there for safekeeping. Now I'm looking for them it's not
an obvious place at all. Then I have to find my mobile, which
is what I have to do every time I leave anywhere. Of course, if
I used one of those holster things to put it in, I wouldn't have
this problem and I would always know where it was, but one

has *some* pride. I remind the children again to feed cat and dog, then leave a note for the cleaner and ask *her* to feed the cat and dog. I remind Grumpy he is picking up kids at 5.30 and that he musn't be late, and can he remember to pick up some food from Tesco's as there's nothing in, especially bread – brown and white, please. I make a mental note to text him a reminder at 5.00.

SETTING OFF

I drive the children to school with Radio 1 playing, as they all refuse to listen to Terry Wogan on Radio 2, which would obviously be my preferred station. Radio 1 smothers its news with funky music because, unlike the programme, it knows that no one listens to the news and thinks that by putting the funky disco stuff under it you're going to be more interested. In fact, it just means that even if you were interested in it, you wouldn't be able to hear it. I also get annoyed at the DJ, who doesn't seem able to articulate any words properly, let alone say something interesting. Some mornings I don't even like his regional accent, which I am certain that he's exaggerating.

In the car Youngest Daughter wants to talk about her next birthday party and who she should invite. Jessica didn't ask her, and she fell out with Sara yesterday, and Anna's ganged up with Christie, so that leaves only Kirsty. You'd have to send Special Branch into the playground with undercover cameras and a hide to find out what actually happens – it all gets so complicated. The girls seem to use birthday parties as a way of telling each other whether they're friends, best friends, joint best friends, old best friends, new best friends or enemies. Reminds me of the canteen at work, come to think of it.

I need to fill up the car with petrol as Grumpy has left it empty again. The whole dreary business of filling the car is so annoying. You pull up and the pump won't reach, or the petrol cap is on the wrong side and you have to repark. Why can't they put petrol caps on both sides of the car? And car maintenance – that doesn't get any easier with new technology: there's all that ghastly business of checking the tyre pressure or filling up with oil. (It took me ages to get the hang of topping up the oil when I got my first car. I assumed that because you *checked* it via the dipstick hole, you topped it up in the same place. I couldn't work out why no one else spilt more than half the oil on the floor, or had to stand on a chair to get the stream thin enough to fit into the hole.)

It's all so much more effort than in the old days, when you pulled up and a pump attendant filled your car and checked your tyre pressure for you. They don't even do the squeezy on the windscreen thing that they do on the Continent (as we called it before the EU).

I drop off the children, worry about them crossing the road, and whether Teenage Daughter is going to get frozen out again by her next-to-last best friend and won't have anyone to sit next to on the coach. The school has issued a million edicts about which way round parents are supposed to drive when they drop their kids off at school, to avoid the gridlock, but still two or three parents (invariably in the biggest, blackest Range Rovers) go the wrong way round because they want to be facing the other way at the end. As a result, the whole thing is always gridlock, with people not budging. On a bad day they get out of their cars and stand in the road with their arms crossed, or hoot their horns and get close to killing someone.

The coach for the school trip is sitting outside the school gate (facing the wrong way according to the school rules – you might know) with its engine on and belching out black smoke, which it's probably been doing for a good 20 minutes, because the school obviously books the cheapest coach possible. So there it sits, pumping out its toxic fumes, which I'm told is illegal: sitting in a parked vehicle and keeping the engine on is actually illegal. So I get out and tap on the window to tell the driver. He looks at me as if to say, 'You poor, sad woman,' and doesn't even say, 'Yes, I can see why this is annoying, but I wanted to listen to my Gene Pitney CD.' He just puts his window up so he can't hear me. When someone does this sort of thing it is bound to ratchet up the rage.

I kicked a bus stop once, I got so angry. If someone had agreed with me and said, 'Yes, isn't this annoying? There are no buses and we've been waiting for half an hour,' I would have calmed down.

Michele Hanson

INFORMATION OVERLOAD

I put my mobile on and play back the messages. It tells me every single time, 'These messages will be deleted within the next 48 hours. To save the message press 2, to delete the message press 4.' Yes, I know that. Unless it's the first-ever time I pick it up to use it, or unless it's not my mobile as I've nicked it, this information is just *too much*. It wastes my time, about 20 seconds each time so, say I listen to my voicemail three times a day, that's a minute a day, nearly half an hour a month listening to this pointless message. But I have no choice but to listen to it, I can't even fast forward it like those maddening information lines for the cinema showing times, which have recently got much better. You can now shout, 'Stop!' during a description of a film that you don't want to see and it skips on to the next one automatically. This is marvellous(ish), although, alas, it is not applicable to real life. If only, when someone was boring you rigid or annoying you totally, if only you could shout, 'Stop!' and they would move on to the next subject. I have started trying it out as a technique among family and friends and feel it could catch on.

Equally, can people stop telling me what is perfectly obvious? We all know quite well how to leave messages on people's phones, thank you very much. So please when I try to leave you a message, please do not have stupid long instructions stating the obvious that I have to listen to first, such as, 'Please leave the date and time you called, your name and a short message [what if I want to leave a *long* message – I always leave one on purpose to annoy them] after the beep.' Yes, yes, yes, we know all that shit. Let's just hear the beep and get on with it. At least people have stopped doing those irritating personalised messages, with their kids reading cute messages or with some stupid music in the background.

The thing about too much information is that it holds me up. And the thing about getting older is that you become acutely aware that time is something you have little of. Wasting time is no longer just a niggle, or an inconvenience; it's a matter – literally – of life and death.

On my way to work there's a big sign that I pass most days and it annoys me every time. It tells me there are 1776 car parking spaces left at the North Car Park in the centre of town. First of all, who's counting them, and am I paying for them to be counted? And second, what is the point? Too much information again because if there are 1776 spaces left, there would have to be one almighty rush into the centre of town for that in any way to be *useful* information. That annoying bloke on Radio 1 would have to have made an announcement saying there's £1 million in £20 notes wafting around the centre of town – get there as soon as you can. And even if the sign got down to the last ten spaces, it might be useful to know if the sign were on the front of the car park itself, but not here on a dual carriageway some 2 miles from the car park. And if it was down to the last ten spaces, you'd think to yourself that you wouldn't risk it as ten other people might just get there first. See that's the sort of thing I spend my time getting all grumped up about. And breathe …

I get out the hands-free set and it slides on to the floor under my feet while I'm going round a roundabout – great. So I stretch down and get it, then fiddle about and eventually poke the blooming thing in my ear. I ring the mother of one of the girls' friends to arrange a play date on Saturday so that I can write the report that is overdue at work and have some time to get ahead. I leave a message.

Then I ring the plumber to ask when he is coming round to fix the bathroom leak. Ring the mother-in-law to remind her that she is picking up the children from swimming and judo on

Thursday. She has forgotten and asks me to remind her on Wednesday.

Midweek is on Radio 4, with a load of celebrities. Yes, strange as it may seem, quite a lot of celebrities make me grumpy. People who are seemingly raking it in because they once did a Scottish dance in the nude on *Big Brother*, or have shagged someone who is good at kicking balls around on a pitch. Or celebrities who endlessly tell us their secrets for looking and feeling young. People like Helen Mirren who looks maddeningly good for her age, and others who show off that they've been at it all night and then twice again before breakfast, and claim it keeps them looking 35. Is there any need to shove it down our throats, as it were?

Then there are all those queeny celebs – usually musicians – which is probably overstating their talent in the first place: people like Celine Dion or Cher, who don't 'do' stairs, people like Elton John, who need a certain type of lily in their dressing room, or celebrities who are so rich that they can close Harrods for a morning to buy some handkerchiefs, while the rest of us have to get on with real life and be done with it.

The media industry feeds on the celebrity frenzy. Magazines such as *Heat, Hello, OK, Closer* or *Further Away*, or some such nonsense, are all disgracefully stupid. All full of ridiculous shots of not very famous people caught on camera picking their nose, eating a hot dog in public or wearing some not very nice clothes. Shock horror. Either that or they have put on a pound, or taken off a pound – big, big news, that one. Then there are all the stupid glamour picture stories – weddings with endless podgy bridesmaids, and the bride's father trying to hide his tattoos and beer belly. You can imagine the stylist turning up at their houses with tasteful cereal bowls and scatter cushions to make their very tasteless house look wonderful.

With some people, such as footballers, they probably have to move in for a couple of days. Never mind 'chuck out your chintz', they probably have to get the removal van in. Still, once they've artfully arranged a vase of twigs that they've had the curling tongs on, and they've put out some muesli and told everyone to hold their tummies in (except for Jade, who doesn't bother to hold it in at all), they look respectable.

Celebrity culling could be an idea. Like they do with deer. Just getting rid of some of the more irritating ones to thin out their swelling numbers. People like Camilla, who lives the life of Riley and has stupid hair, or Brian Sewell, who is unspeakably stuck up, or Andrew Lloyd Webber who is simply too ugly and too rich. But there are one or two celebrities that I have warmed to with time. People such as Michael Winner, who I loathed for years, with his stupid blazer and top pocket hanky spilling out and his ridiculously pompous restaurant column, but now I see him in those chirpy little insurance ads and quite like him. Like him more than that nice man who used to be on *Z Cars*. And I liked *him* a lot.

ARRIVAL

No change for the parking meter, so I go to buy a *Daily Mail* to get some change. Michael Winner is on the front page wearing his flouncy hanky and looking pleased with himself. Have gone off him. Can't find anywhere to park. Someone texts me but I can't read it without my specs. Some days I just wish I could go back to being a kid and do some join-the-dots all morning, or maybe something a bit more challenging, such as spot the difference. Being a grown-up is so much more difficult than I expected.

I find parking very annoying now. I don't think I used to. I think I used to just, well, park. Now every multistorey is, in its own way, extremely annoying: either the pay and display machine is a half-mile hike away from the cars, or the machines don't work, or people use the stairwells as latrines, or the way they make you drive round them is stupid. But more than that, I find myself being ridiculously choosy about which space to park in. I reject dozens before I plump for one. They're too near the wall, or too near the next car, or the car next door is a bit lopsided, or reversing out of it looks a bit too challenging. Other people just seem to swing in, but I end up on level five and still haven't found one that is just right. I'm getting like my dad in this respect: he used to do that. Sometimes he would start parking in a space, then spot another one that looked better – roomier – so he'd re-park, and the whole thing would take hours. Of course, once you come back at the end of the day, the whole terrain has changed anyway, and the space you thought looked a doddle to get out of is now surrounded by cars all parked in a hurry, and you have to climb over the gearstick to get into the car at all. I put the parking sticker on, knowing that however carefully I do it, a sticky mess will be left behind and I will have to spend half an hour with a green scourer one Saturday morning getting all the little blighters off. If I get a parking ticket, the worst bit is not the fine, though the money is a drag, that's for sure, but the glue that sticks the ticket to the windscreen: it's the stickiest glue on earth and takes industrial cleaning to remove. In fact, the mess it leaves behind never goes completely, and you have it there as an indelible reminder of your stupidity until you sell the car.

Eventually I get to the first meeting at work. People are kissing one another. I don't mean they're snogging – I mean we all have to do the kissy-kissy thing with the man from head office, like we're old friends. What a stupid waste of time this has become. We join the EU and suddenly you can't just say

'How do you do' or shake someone's hand; you have to do a kiss on each cheek, and is it one or two, right or left first? You don't know where you are with it. The meeting is a total waste of time, and I come out with a list of three things to do, all of which I know will come to nothing and waste more time.

Next is half an hour of coffee and calls in the comparative calm of office life. I rewrite my list. Straight into best. Nice new page of A4 lined pad.

THAT DOES NOT COMPUTE

I log on at my desk. Why don't computers ever work for long? They work for about five minutes, then start sending you stupid attention-seeking messages that make no sense at all, for example: 'The path "I" cannot be found. Verify that you have access to this location and try again, or try to find the installation package "NOwCEMSi".' Oh, bog off.

You switch off and reboot and all this sort of thing. I tell you, I have felt sometimes like opening up the window and hurling my computer out, and the only reason I don't do so is concern for the people down below. Because if you're going to be brained, please not by a computer.

Ann Widdecombe

You turn them off, give them a rest, sometimes overnight, whisper sweet nothings to them, and they just continue to misbehave.

I get in a complete rage with the computer. I get all hot, my hair is standing on end, I look like a clown trying to control myself, shouting, 'You fucking thing.' Then I get up and walk away, and the bloody egg-timer on the screen is still there.

Nina Myskow

There should be a smack or bite button.

Computers are for writing, shopping and sending and receiving emails. Girls' computers anyway. And I really resent it when occasionally mine tries to take over my life and little signs will pop up saying things like, 'We have located this software that we'd like to update.' Go away. I'm doing something else, I'm on Ebay, I'm buying vintage shoes … I know if I did click that button it's going to take eight or nine hours, then it will crash before it's finished and it will say 'Sorry, we didn't manage to finish this thing, so could you do it again tomorrow?' No, I don't want to do that. Go away.

Kathryn Flett

Even when you do tell them that you don't want to update anything, they still don't let it lie. They say, '*When* would you like me to remind you about this again?' There just isn't an option that says 'never', so you have to click the one that says once every 24 hours, and then you are plagued with the message forever more.

Unlike most women of my generation, I do love computers, but I get terribly angry when it freezes, you know it freezes and sends you messages saying you have committed an illegal action. Sorry, I am sitting here minding my own business. I have done nothing wrong. It's you that has frozen. Something has gone wrong in your innards. How dare you blame me.

Sheila Hancock

And the email junk. There must be at least five every time I log on at the moment, advertising Viagra or penis extensions. They might at least advertise a spot of female porn. Now that might be worth a look. All these revolutions in technology and still no one has invented something that stops the shower curtain sticking to you. Or some wonder pill that means you can eat as many Mars bars as you like and won't put on any weight. Who should I write to, I wonder?

And what about iPods – the latest thing? It's not in the freezer section, where it sounds as if it should be, but is the cleverest, poshest sound system ever – so small that it fits into the gap in your front teeth.

It's some sort of mini jukebox. It's like a Sony Walkman, which has got, as far as I can tell, all the songs you have ever wanted to listen to. Can I just say my father has an iPod. He's got the time, he's got the manual, he's a man, he can do iPods. I can't do them. I'm a middle-aged woman and I'm grumpy.

Kathryn Flett

Using an iPod means you can walk around Sainsbury's plugged into 3000 tracks at any one time. So when you are in front of the 12 sorts of baked beans you can be choosing between 3000 music tracks at the same time. Neat!

Some people seem to manage this whole computer bit so

much better than I do. The cleverest people on the planet are able to type the address on a letter and fold it so that it is showing in the right place through the window. The rest of us type the letter six times before we get it right. Even cleverer people manage to master the art of printing out labels with all their friends' and family's addresses for their Christmas card envelopes. One flick of the switch and they are done, having a sit-down with a mince pie while the rest of us are writing them all out by hand, slaving over them all night. The nearest I got to it was one year when I managed to print them all out, but the addresses were astride two labels, so I threw them in the bin like a four-year-old and sulked.

Filling in forms online is also a nightmare for someone as grumpy as me. In fact, forms generally get me down in a big way. It's like the tax returns you have to do yourself now. Personal admin is bad enough, but filling in the tax form takes me a whole day. And why are there never options such as 'depends' or 'sometimes'? The accompanying notes are as big as the phone directory, so obviously I can't be bothered to read them quietly and sensibly because there are too many other things I would prefer to be doing with my time. This probably explains why last year my tax return was posted back to me querying the figure in box 3E, since I had put a five-figure sum in it, and they were a bit confused because 3E is the box where you had to add up all your gratuities or tips if you are a waitress or something. I had put £26,000 in that box by mistake. They must have thought I was running a high-class brothel.

I rush to the gym at lunchtime and do ten minutes on the treadmill. Lunch used to be for lunch. Now we all have to cram some sport into our already crowded day. Our mothers scampered about at their health and beauty class once a week, or did a bit of cycling to get the groceries, but now we have to spend every spare millisecond at the gym. Well, we're supposed to.

Exercise is for schoolgirls, and it's compulsory. I don't do exercise, therefore I have cellulite.

Kathryn Flett

Back to the relative calm of office life, and for about three hours I achieve a lot of crossings-out on the list, which is code for 'job satisfaction'.

Get home and on to the Tesco website since Grumpy has texted to say he is working late and can't get to the shops. It takes me about 30 minutes fiddling about to view which cherry tomatoes and which pasta to buy, and then I've lost my password and have to go through the virtual checkout as a new customer, which takes forever, and the stupid thing times out on me just as I am getting to the delivery times. Total waste of half an hour, and I still have to go to the actual supermarket.

Computers were meant to make our lives so much easier, supposed to give us so much more time to loll about, but somehow all they seem to make us do is take on more tasks, and have less time to just sit down, enjoy life and do nothing. Doing nothing – now there's a novelty. Then someone we know dies and we all stop, jaws dropped, as if no one had ever told us that time was going to actually *run out*. Someone gets up at the funeral and reads that famous poem 'Funeral Blues' from *Four Weddings and a Funeral*, and we all look as if it's the first we've heard that yes, we do eventually run out of time.

IT'S A HARD LIFE

Our parents seemed to have much more time – time just to sit by the fire or listen to *The Archers* or *The Clitheroe Kid*, or to visit Auntie Marjorie. Their parents – if the poor sods weren't sitting in a trench somewhere with a rifle or holding a ration book in their hand – also had more time. How did that work, then? I guess they washed and blow-dried their hair less, went to Pilates and Majorca less. They didn't try to commute 200 miles a day, they didn't try to do dinner parties for 12, or change the decor in their living room every two years, or work out of an office in Leeds and London simultaneously. We rush about and wear ourselves out, then a Center Parcs ad comes on the telly to tell us to make sure we have more time to sit and stare at a lake or a flower, which makes us even more stressed out and, worse than that, makes us feel trapped on the hamster treadmill that is our lives. It's not even as if Center Parc holidays are the least bit relaxing. I'm not saying they don't have their good points (I'm not stupid – they'll sue me or something), but queuing to put your knickers in a locker along with 1000 other people and being in a telephone queue to book the only badminton court left at 8.30 on a Sunday morning is not my idea of relaxation.

Even cameras are irritating. Digital cameras seem marvellous until you realise that you have to log on, download and then transfer all the shots to CD, then you might want to print them on your computer, which involves yet more hours and hours and hours of fiddling about with printers, and downloading, and special paper and, oh my God. I don't want to spend the weekend doing that. What's wrong with just taking the film to Boots and going back a week later when it's developed?

Ann Widdecombe has her own theory about the stress that seems to have got much worse over the last couple of decades:

I think a lot of stress is self-imposed. Some of life's problems are thrown at one, but I think people now have a completely false image of what they should be, and this is measured not by what they should be, but by what they must have. People are always striving for the next thing. You want your house and then you want a bigger house and you must have the latest model of car. And you must have the latest model of washing machine. And that creates enormous stress. You don't get all that by gently contemplating the world. You get all that by striving and competing with the world, and of course that sort of stress is entirely self-induced.

Ann Widdecombe

Then all the technology takes up so much of your time to maintain, cajole and generally nanny. You have to charge it all up and make sure you have all the right dooberries. I've lost count of how many times I have lugged my laptop over to the other side of the world and spent most of the first day trying to log on in my room. Either the modem or the connection thingy or the control panel needs changing, so in the end you just lug it all back home again, having collected a backlog of paperwork that will take you an entire weekend at home to sort out. Most of us apparently still can't programme our video recorders, and how long have we been using them? About 30 years. So what hope is there for us?

WHINGING IS GOOD FOR YOU

Is it any wonder, then, that we start making formal complaints? We make complaining into an art form. We write to the manager or the chief executive, demanding that something is changed. It's not enough to glare at total strangers or be sarky, or get your fellow passengers on your side. You put pen to paper. You know it's going to end in tears and sick, but you enter into a correspondence to get it all off your chest and out of your system. You're on your way to green biro land.

I do write a hell of a lot of letters of complaint. I haven't really got time to do it, but I find it gets rid of some of my rage.

Sheila Hancock

Of course, if you get into complaining big time, it culminates in your buying something that puts you firmly into Victor Meldrew territory. Something that is entirely and utterly and totally bad for your image – a personal shredder. Mind you, they do make a rather satisfactory noise as the stuff goes through.

We are simply subject to too much information all round. If it's not intimate details of Jordan's love life, or the gory details of Tamara Beckwith's colonic irrigation kick, then it's stupid information you don't want – or could never imagine wanting – on your new watch. Like it tells you when it's high tide in Singapore, or when All Saints' Day falls the year after next. It clogs up your brain and makes your head hurt. Even the simplest egg-timer comes with a manual that could keep you busy in 12 languages for the best part of a weekend. If you really wanted to know the exact function of every single button or dial in your car or on your CD player, you'd need to go on a course, not read a manual. Then you'd need a refresher course six months later, but by then they'd have changed the model anyway. I don't want all this information. I just want to buy a watch that tells the time, in my time zone, without me needing to put my specs on, and without having to waste any time working out how to get the battery changed or get the stupid thing going in the first place. In fact, I'd rather pay more for one that didn't give me all that information. Here's a tip, everyone: charge us more and give us less. It'll catch on, I promise you.

When I get to Tesco's in person, I tear around the place like a mad thing, wanting to shove people out of the way, and getting angry about some of the items they've moved. In most situations like this I feel that I want to take over, to reorganise it all, get a whistle round my neck and simply order everybody around like a commander-in-chief. I fancy one of those platforms like they have on traffic junctions in India, where I could police the nine-items-or-fewer queue, blow my whistle at people and publicly humiliate the ones who don't put the 'Next customer, please' divider on the belt, and get the whole business moving much faster. If it means gunning down the odd pensioner who takes too long to get their money out, then so be it. I am in a hurry and I don't care who knows it. I'm the same in post-office queues, restaurants, hotels, everything. I want to take over and do it my way.

I start making tea like I'm on some TV show, where the one who does it fastest gets a holiday for two in the Caribbean. I rush around opening freezer, fridge and cupboards with the efficiency of a time and motion expert, and produce baked potatoes with cheese and salad in about 18 minutes flat. Grumpy would take about an hour to do it, as he is incapable of doing more than one task at once. I've got the washing out of the machine, made the beds that weren't made this morning, because although they are about to be got into again, that's not the point, walked the dog, fed the cat, read the post, sorted out the things needed at domestic science tomorrow, and all in 40 minutes flat. But I feel like shit. When the children were smaller this would have been called quality time – time for me to read them a story or help them do a painting while I simultaneously make a cheese soufflé and open some emails. These days the kids are glued to the telly watching unspeakable rubbishy sitcoms from America on Sky TV. They've seen so many episodes of *Friends* that they talk about dialling 911 not 999, or they talk about high school, and do all that oh-my-God business all the time. I despair.

TV TIME

While ironing for tomorrow, I indulge in a bit of *Richard and Judy*. I'm not listening to anything they're saying, but wonder – like everyone else, I would imagine – whether they are still really an item or not. He constantly interrupts her on screen, which must be maddening. I feel very sorry for her, but on the other hand, I do love the clip of her at the awards ceremony with her bra showing. I love it when they show it again; in fact, I don't tire of it. If they sold it on a loop, like the images of a roaring fire or a calming seascape, I'd buy one.

Once the kids are in bed, and I've had a glass of wine and something to eat with Grumpy, there's a window of about 45 minutes when I can flop and watch something on the telly. And, yes, you guessed it, there's a lot of it that narks me. Everything is sexed up and souped up to death, so they constantly recap, tease up and recap again. Sometimes they recap what you just saw in the recap, and then go to a commercial break before anything new has actually happened. It's enough to give you Alzheimer's. They've even messed about with wildlife programmes. You thought you knew where you were with them: David Attenborough would appear in his trusty beige trousers and pale blue shirt and tell you something amazing. You could sit and watch it with the family and come away feeling you had learnt something. Now they even have to jazz those up, and someone's decided that Bill Oddie is really, really wild, really, really cool, and it all has to be LIVE! with an exclamation mark at the end of it. But it is *so* not cool and *so* not wild. Bring back *Animal Magic*. And, by the way, exclamation marks! Annoy me! Too!

But the thing that annoys me most on telly is all the sport. I don't care if I never see a golf tournament, a snooker match or a rugby international ever in my entire life. OK, so I don't

mind the odd bit of the Cup Final – where you hear them sing
'Abide with Me' and get a bit teary – but why does it all have to
take over our lives so? Why can't people channel their energies
into something a bit more meaningful? It's just that everyone
seems to think it's so very important, and it's not. The moment
we're in the final 40 of anything – even tiddlywinks – the
entire TV schedule has to be refashioned to accommodate it.
You get yourself five minutes and the chance to catch up on a
bit of *Corrie* or *EastEnders*, and the whole thing has been
shunted back to 10.30 p.m. (extra time permitting), by which
time I will almost certainly have nodded off. Then they have to
analyse the game to the point where even Gary Lineker looks a
bit bored with it. If you want to watch sport, get yourself Sky
and be done with it so that the rest of us can get on with
normality, that's what I say.

Then there are hundreds of retrospectives about
programmes that weren't very good in the first place, or only
went out five years ago, so we get another ghastly dose of
comedy that's not funny – *The Goodies, Benny Hill, The Goons* …
They were never funny, so why celebrate them now? Do you
know *anyone normal* who found *The Goons* funny? Prince
Charles, apparently. That explains a lot.

My attitude to television has very slowly shifted from
finding the most irresponsible programmes funny, to being
more moral and outraged. More aware of people's feelings
being hurt, of their lives being wrung out and ruined for a
cheap laugh. I thought Louis Theroux hugely entertaining until
he got all devious with the marvellous Ann Widdecombe, trying
to make her look silly with her cuddly toys and get prurient
shots of her bedroom. I thought that wasn't right. And whilst
I can see that some of the antics that Michael Jackson gets up
to at his ranch are, to say the least, odd, I could also see that
Martin Bashir was extremely dishonest and gave the impression

of making a very different film from the one that was transmitted. And what about those poor families on *Wife Swap*? It must seem like such a good idea at the time, to be on the telly, to get a bit famous for a few weeks, but how many families have suffered a serious blip as a result, for our entertainment? How many kids saw their own parents as selfish adults who didn't have time to play with them, didn't have time to nurture them and love them as much as they could have done, as a result of seeing their family contrasted with one that is entirely more wholesome, more middle-class? Call me old-fashioned, but I think real life is more important than telly.

AND SO TO BED

I go to bed with my little pile of catalogues that have come through the door. It's my bedtime routine – something I look forward to, something that I know will round off my day. I might browse through some of the new Lakeland knick-knacks, noticing that they've just brought in a neat plastic container for holding two biscuits. They look like those awful things they sell to put Tampax in your handbag – great big pink holders designed to disguise the fact that you might need some sanitary products, but instead actively advertise it so that you can see it at 100 yards. I tick the biscuit holder, not star it, which means that I quite like it, but might not buy it. You'd only eat your two biscuits and want another one, but the packet would be back at home, so you'd have this funny mini-frisbee in your bag all day. Then again, it would stop you eating more than two biscuits, and wrapping biscuits in cling film and putting them in your bag doesn't really work, so they've obviously spotted a gap in the market. It's a good way to get off to sleep.

CHAPTER ELEVEN

Life's a bitch and then you're dead

UNTIL I GOT TO THIRTY, death was something that was inconceivably far off in the future; it was not really going to happen at all. I could puff away at a packet of Rothmans a day and remain invincible. I could worry about dying later, a *lot* later. Then someone you love dies, and suddenly it feels like it matters. Some smart Alec tells you that you can work out where you are in your life by imagining it as one year. In my case I've reached about late September, which is terrifying. I shall still be trying to get the hang of it all, and it'll all be over. I'm now so old that I can remember the start of colour TV, and can sing all the early ad campaigns, such as 'The Esso sign means happy motoring' or 'A thousand and one cleans a big, big carpet' – that sort of useless rubbish. That's how old I am. Old.

I've always been a terrible daydreamer, but I'm starting to fantasise about my own funeral. The more funerals I go to, the more I start to ponder the details of my own. But recently it's become more serious than that: I've started to think quite hard about it. I don't mean simply in terms of whether I'll plump for burial or cremation, but almost looking forward to it. To wish I could be there, as it were. I let my imagination run riot, pondering the the minute details of the event and wallowing in self-pity and self-indulgence, thinking just how much my family and friends will weep and wail for me when I'm newly gone. And since the crematorium's page of remembrance will fall open on my name only a measly once a year, my funeral will need to be truly memorable, a huge one-off, a lasting mark in the world. I wonder about hiring a biplane to write my epitaph in the sky, as they do at the seaside to advertise the new Aldi and stuff – something like 'Judith Holder: the one and only' or 'Judith Holder: didn't you just love her' – but it would be just my luck for it to be too foggy to fly, and anyway it's a bit, well, naff. It all stems from a childish desire to make people feel sorry they were ever horrid to me, or ever took me for granted.

I know what's sparked it off. I drove through the village last week to find that the entire place had been taken over by a funeral. Someone who was obviously very popular. The whole village was awash with yellow RAC car park and diversion signs. The thing that stopped me in my tracks, chilled me to the bone, was the sign saying OVERFLOW CAR PARK. The deceased was evidently so popular, so significant, so beloved that the guest list not only filled the church car park and spilled

over into the pay and display, but even warranted an entire
field to be designated as an overflow car park. A gasp of
anxiety escaped my lips: how many people will be at my
funeral? And, crucially, will it necessitate an overflow, or fit
snugly into the small car park behind the church?

Should I go for somewhere with a particularly small car
park? Avoid the problem occurring in the first place? A quick
headcount of the likely invitees reveals that it all very much
depends on *when* I die. Leave it too long and, although I might
have made one or two new acquaintances at the bingo and
watercolour classes, some of the current more *compos mentis*
possibles may well have pegged it themselves. Leave it until my
80s, and the guest list might just consist of the couple who live
over the road, with the undertakers themselves having to fill up
some of the pews. I'm trying to be optimistic. What if I kick
the bucket in August and everyone's away on holiday? Maybe
it would be an idea to go for a smart memorial service instead
… send out the invites now with an RSVP and a questionnaire
asking when would be the most convenient time of year –
morning or afternoon, evening or weekend? Might be better
than leaving the whole thing to chance. Yes, best to get
something pencilled in now; that way I can drum up lots of
support and all-important cars. Then no one will be in any
doubt as to just how popular and special I was. Am.

This sort of fantasy is so utterly immature. It's just like the
one I indulged in as a child – the one that went: if I left home
in a strop after a row with Mum and Dad, they would be *so*
worried and *so* sorry. That'd show them. I can only assume
that this adolescent fantasy is all part of being a middle-aged
mother with Teenage Daughter who treats me like a piece of
dog poo. All part of being married to a middle-aged man who
doesn't notice when I've had my hair cut, or when I wear an
entirely new outfit … probably something to do with being

middle-aged, invisible and taken for granted. No wonder
Wendy Craig's character in *Butterflies* was tempted to have
affairs. Some hope. You should see our milkman.

As for the funeral itself – this is interesting food for thought
on the fantasy front. I don't want any of this sober, buttoned-
up nonsense. Full-blown weeping and wailing is more up my
street. I want people to be unable to contain themselves,
clutching sodden pieces of tissue, so the choice of hymns is
crucial – something really heart-breaking, such as 'Little
Donkey' or 'We Plough the Fields and Scatter'. They always
get people going, swelling up their faces and making them look
like they've gone six rounds in the boxing ring. There'll be
some tear gas standing by in case they don't do the trick. Some
poetry perhaps – maybe a specially composed verse from one
of the Mother's Day cards that the girls made for me when
they were young. And still liked me. Some people might have
to go outside to compose themselves after that bit.

Next come some psalm readings, ideally by that nice vicar
on 'Thought for the Day'. Then there's pop music: shall I go
for some Steely Dan or Stevie Wonder? A post-modern ironic
version of 'My Way' might be stylish, with some huge photos
of me and the family in the background. And naturally I shall
go to town with a message I will write for the occasion and
leave in a strategic place: TO BE READ AT MY FUNERAL.
I can enjoy poring over and perfecting the text of this during
the coming years. Words to haunt my friends and family from
beyond the grave. Words in particular to take the wind out of
Teenage Daughter and Youngest Daughter and for them to
realise that I am a great deal better as a mother than they
thought. At least lots of other people loved and adored me, so
I can't have been all *that* bad.

Then there's the will. The tried and tested method of
stating your case and getting your message across with no

answering back at all. Leave the teenager's legacy with lots of strings attached, such as make it payable only if she brushes her hair off her face into a velvet Alice band, wears Start-rite shoes and her school skirt on the knee. The choice is hers, then. I told you it was a fantasy. Or I could stipulate that the life insurance only pays out to Grumpy if he folds the towels neatly in the bathroom after he's had a shower. Or I could demand that people scale the side of Scapa Fell to distribute my ashes … and revisit there once a year on the anniversary of my death. In January. You can see how the whole thing starts to become enjoyable.

I lie on the sofa feeling very sorry for myself and ask Grumpy if he'll cry much at my funeral. He looks a bit puzzled and says it would depend on how well Man U were doing at the time. No one seems to take me seriously.

Perhaps mine is a universal fantasy, and it may explain why people of my age throw themselves so enthusiastically into voluntary work, the Rotary Club or organising the Harvest Supper. That way everyone in the village is going to say what a lovely person you were, and make an effort to show up on the all-important day. I may not be in the specially named park bench or hospital ward category (I draw the line at being on the local council), but with any luck at the very least the butcher might be closed for the day of my funeral, with a card in the window saying 'CLOSED DUE TO JUDITH HOLDER'S FUNERAL'. As long as I keep buying his black pudding at any rate. It may not be huge TV screens relaying the action in the crematorium to the crowds in Hyde Park, but it's a start.

Pity there isn't a way of my being there to see it.

I'm spending more and more time on this kind of self-indulgent nonsense. I drive down the motorway and I wonder what would happen if I turned the wheel just a couple of degrees to the left when I go under the bridges, or how much of a turn it would take for me to crash into the barrier. I'm almost tempted to try, just for the hell of it, to see how much it would hurt, what it would feel like, but then you'd feel a complete nana.

Maybe some good old-fashioned religion would be helpful, some straightforward rules to live by instead of all this flailing about, trying to make some sense out of why we're here and what happens to us when we're gone. We build secular shrines at the roadside where someone has been run over, lighting candles and tying indifferent bunches of flowers to the railings to remind everyone on an hourly basis that their lives could at any moment be cut short. It's not very – well – helpful really, and then they go all neglected and horrid, which just underlines the fact that once you're gone, you're gone, and nothing – not even a few bunches of flowers – is going to help anybody bring you back.

As I get older I feel more and more receptive to religion. I like 'Thought for the Day' on the radio, and I find myself enjoying stirring hymns – don't even turn them off any more. But being a Christian is so – well, unfashionable. You can be a Buddhist, a feng shuist, or whatever they call themselves, you can go round in orange robes and jangle cubes of crystal round your neck and people will give you some respect, but if you say you're a Christian you are written off as a nerd or an eccentric.

We place no emphasis now on the spiritual. We sneer at the spiritual. We sneer at Christianity. We sneer at any concept of self-restraint.
Ann Widdecombe

But at the risk of sounding very old-fashioned indeed, I think if we all lived by Christian values, the world might be a considerably nicer place. I just can't help thinking that if God *did* make the world, he might have been called away on urgent business and be due back any minute now to sort out the mess we've all made of it.

Acknowledgements

Thanks to the fabulous celebrity grumpees who were good enough to share their grump with the nation on the TV series, and without whose wit and wisdom this book would not have happened – Jilly Cooper, Annette Crosbie, Jenny Eclair, Kathryn Flett, Bonnie Greer, Professor Germaine Greer, Michele Hanson, Lesley Joseph, Dillie Keane, India Knight, Angie LeMar, Maureen Lipman, Nina Myskow, Jane Moore, Linda Robson, Janet Street Porter, Jenni Trent Hughes, Arabella Weir and Rt Hon Ann Widdecombe MP. Thanks to Sheila Hancock and the John Thaw Foundation for her support, and to Maureen Lipman for writing the foreword. Thanks to Stuart Prebble of Liberty Bell Productions whose brilliant idea *Grumpy Old Men* was, and who made it all right – even a little bit cool – to be grumpy. Thanks to Jo Clinton Davies and Maxine Watson at the BBC for realising that women could be as grumpy as men – if not more so! I am indebted to the production team who worked with me on the BBC series – especially Claire Storey, Chris Sutcliffe, Susan Manning, Fahima Chowdhury, Jules Williamson and Caroline Broome. Thanks also to the brilliant team at BBC Books – Shirley Patton, Sarah Reece and Linda Blakemore – who have been among the least grumpy people I've met. And thanks to my fellow Grumpy Old Women, who have trod the same path at the same time and who have encouraged me and made me laugh a lot on the way – Martine Carassik, Jane Dammers, Judith Derbyshire, Anne Leuchars, Jill Scrimshaw and Victoria Wood. Thanks to my mother, Jean Holder, for being such a good sport, and last but not least, thanks to my very own Grumpy Old Man, Mike Parker, who has – with his overall domestic incompetence – provided me with a certain amount of material for this book, but who – let's face it – has to put up with living with a grump like me. But then, like most middle-aged women, I make up for it in so many different and gorgeous ways …

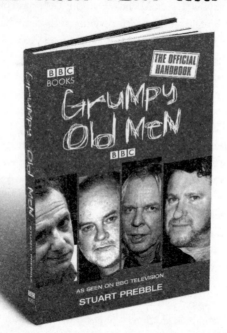